LEADERSHIP
INSIGHTS

FOR EMERGING LEADERS
AND THOSE INVESTING IN THEM

STEVE MOORE
FOREWORD BY TIM ELMORE

Leadership Insights for Emerging Leaders and Those Investing in Them

Published by Top Flight Leadership, Fort Worth, Texas

Unless otherwise noted, all Bible verses are taken from the HOLY BIBLE: NEW INTERNATIONAL VERSION (c) 1986 by Holman Bible Publishers, Nashville, Tennessee.

ISBN: 0-9711942-3-8
Library of Congress Control Number: 2002092311

Cover Design: James Gerhold
Editing/Interior Layout Design: Kim Kelley

Table of Contents

Foreword

Every now and then, you read a book and feel as though it's more than just a person talking with you. You get the sneaking suspicion it's far deeper than that. You feel something stirring inside of you. The words on the page take on deeper significance. They haunt you. You suddenly realize God is speaking to you, and the book has become a tool in His hands.

That's how this book will strike many of you. My chief concern is that too few will read it. It is a call to a life that is deeper than the one you might be living right now. It is a challenge to live and lead the way Jesus did. It's a challenge to forsake the self-life—the comfortable, fashionable, pleasurable life—and strike out as a pioneer with Him. That's really what leadership is all about. It's choosing to influence instead of merely being influenced by the world around us. It means stepping out of a comfort zone even when it might appear radical to others. It's about finding your passion and gift, and serving in that area, instead of being satisfied with survival.

In this book, Steve Moore challenges you to rethink how you live and lead. The book is simple and straightforward. It's a no-nonsense approach to the subject. In it, you will meet radical leaders from the pages of history… leaders like C. T. Studd, Amy Carmichael, Winston Churchill, and others. If you take their words to heart, they will change you. Steve has a way of interpreting people and events so that others can benefit from them. He's done that for me many times.

I have worked with college students since 1979. Over the last several years, I have focused my attention almost purely on student leadership development. After surveying 3,000 college students on their attitudes toward leadership, I have drawn a few conclusions. First, the real need is to call them back to this kind of leadership development, the kind that begins with the heart, not techniques and mechanics. Second, the real need is to cast a vision for changing the world, not filling a position. Most students avoid leadership positions because they feel those positions aren't legitimate places to make a difference. I believe they can be, if the student in the position can see the big picture of why they are there. The position doesn't make the leader. The leader makes the position. Third, I believe student leaders today are looking for mentors who will help them navigate their way through the process. That's what I think Steve Moore is attempting to do here.

I recommend you not only read this book, but also interact with it. Invite some friends to go through it with you. Allow it to become a comrade as you begin to influence the world you live in. Then act on what you learn. These insights are invitations to a whole new way of life.

Blessings on you as you bless others.

—Tim Elmore
Vice-President of EQUIP

Acknowledgements

I want to say a special thanks to Brooks, Jill, Sarah, Tim, Cheryl, Scott, Dave, Deanna, Dan, David, Daniel, Eric, Khushi, Rosemary, Marty, Rob, Sean, Connie, Trent & Nikki, Bala and Rob.
Thanks for allowing me to speak into your leadership journey through the email version of *Leadership Insights*.
Many of you will go farther and reach higher than I ever dreamed. I hope, in part, because you are standing on my shoulders.

Thanks also to the Top Flight Leadership team for encouraging me to bring these ideas to a wider audience and providing the platform to help young leaders fulfill their God-appointed dreams.

Getting Started

A value that continues to shape my approach to ministry is that more time with less people equals greater Kingdom impact. I believe in the importance of a platform ministry, but I have a deeper commitment to more personally and intentionally invest in a smaller network of people. I believe the increased time I have given to a smaller group of people will ultimately result in greater Kingdom impact since the investment they will make in the lives of others will ripple out across spheres of influence I may never directly touch.

This being said, one of the practical challenges of living out this value is the fact that many of the young leaders I would like to spend more time with are scattered around the world. I've met them as I have traveled to various countries for ministry, or they have gone to the far corners of the earth out of obedience to God's call on their lives. It's simply not possible for me to physically get together with them.

So I decided a few years ago to try to recreate a "more time with less people" approach to ministry via a regular article distributed by email to a small group of young leaders around the world. I called this article *Leadership Insights* and bundled with it a short list of application questions. I required each person on my "subscription list" to respond consistently to the *Leadership Insights* article by interacting with one or more of the ap-plication steps and communicating with me via email. I consistently re-affirmed that not responding to the *Leadership Insights* article for several weeks in a row would be a surefire way of saying "Please take me off your list." In this way, I was able to keep the group size to about twenty young leaders but still make room for newcomers as people dropped off the list.

Over time I began to stockpile a list of articles on various topics affecting younger Christian leaders. Often I would meet a young leader in my travels that asked me a question about a topic I knew I had written about in a *Leadership Insights* article. I routinely answered the question as best I could on the spot and closed by suggesting he or she email me a reminder and I'd send an article that addressed the question in more detail.

Eventually I realized that I had a growing reservoir of articles written specifically to young leaders, most of which had never been read by more than twenty-five people! I found myself rethinking what it means to be a good steward of this information, and the result of that process, along with the input of my *Leadership Insights* subscribers and colleagues at Top Flight Leadership, resulted in the book you now hold in your hands.

Who are these articles for?

The initial core of *Leadership Insights* readers were staff members and interns in a young leader training ministry with whom I served prior to Top Flight Leadership. After joining the staff of Top Flight Leadership, that "subscription list" broadened to include a network of young leaders with whom I had some level of relationship. For the most part they are twentysomething young leaders ranging from college students to church planters, from first-term missionaries to ministry leaders whose focus is training younger leaders.

In short, these articles were written primarily to serious-minded young leaders in the 20–30 age group, on five different continents, in many different settings, who shared a common motivation to grow in their leadership potential. Most of them had a preexisting relationship with me, although a number of subscribers found their way onto my list without anything more than a weekend connection at a retreat or training event where I was speaking.

A smaller number of mature leaders have stuck with *Leadership Insights* because they found the articles helpful in their ministry to train young leaders. Several indigenous leaders around the world have routinely translated and contextualized *Leadership Insights* articles for use in their own publications or training seminars. If a part of your ministry includes developing young leaders, you may find some helpful ideas here as well.

How can I make the most of this resource?

Since there are really two distinct audiences for this material—young leaders and those who work with them—I want to address the issue of making the most of this resource separately for each group.

If you are a young leader...

- *View this as an "on-demand" workshop.* I often hear young leaders lamenting about the fact that they don't get many training opportunities that are specifically focused on their needs. View this book as a conference waiting to happen with twenty-four workshops addressing topics relevant to you as a young leader. When I surveyed the *Leadership Insights* subscriber list, over 80 percent of them said the topics were relevant to where they were at and applicable to their situation. Bottom line—this is not a book you will want to read in one sitting. Make it a part of your growth plan for the year, and attend two "on-demand" workshops each month. Don't go in order; mix things up based on what you want to learn in any given month.

- *Give priority to application.* I mentioned earlier that each article has accompanying application suggestions. Pick at least one or two of them and find a way to apply the ideas the best you can. I know for a fact based on my email-mentoring group that if you interact with this material at more than an intellectual level you will get more out of it. For most of us, it's not what we don't know that holds us back as much as what we do know but never apply. Application deepens assimilation which fuels the desire for more information which takes me right back where I started—another opportunity for application. And so on.

- *Use it as a reference tool down the road.* The titles for each article may not be all that creative but they are intended to reveal the topic so you can refer quickly to an article that speaks to a question that has surfaced in your journey. Inasmuch as I have found these articles helpful follow-up resources for young leaders I've counseled in various settings around the world, you may find the wide range of topics speak into your life at just the right time.

- *Share your thoughts with others in the form of a peer-mentoring group.* Learning can be much more rewarding when you share the journey with a few others in the form of a learning community. This resource lends itself to group study in that you can skip around in the stand-alone articles and rotate the leadership of the group. Hold each other accountable for the application steps. Sharpen your focus with the ideas and perspectives of other young leaders.

- *Subscribe to* Leadership Insights Online *and continue expanding your leadership potential.* If you purchased this book—as opposed to borrowing it from a friend—you are entitled to a free six-month subscription to *Leadership Insights Online* where you will receive twelve additional articles—two per month. You can continue receiving *Leadership Insights Online* with your paid subscription. Just follow the instructions printed on the inside back cover of this book and start receiving your free subscription. (If for some reason you have problems activating your free subscription, please email info@topflight .org or call 866-9LEADER for assistance.)

If you are working with young leaders...

- *Seek to expand your understanding of young leader issues.* As you work through this material you will discover many of these articles hit hard and deal with substantive issues. Be encouraged about the fact there are many young leaders who are ready to move beyond the sex-and-dating talks to real meat. Don't sell your young leaders short by believing they don't care about issues like dealing with failure or managing a crisis or developing a life purpose.

- *Use this as a catalyst for starting a mentoring group.* Buy a few extra copies and invite three or four young leaders to digest this with you. Let them pick the order of the articles and share in the responsibility for leading the group. Hold each other accountable for applying what you learn. Look for those who want to go deeper with a given topic and point them to additional resources.

- *Supplement your existing leadership training.* You may want to pick some of these topics and use the article as a seed for developing your own leadership training session. Teach it with passion and don't worry about telling them where you got it. Just keep investing in the young leaders God has entrusted to you.

- *Reprint an article that you really like in your own publication.* That's right. Reprint it. You have our permission. Just be sure to include the following tag line with your article:

  This article is reprinted from the book *Leadership Insights,* with permission from Steve Moore and Top Flight Leadership. To purchase *Leadership Insights* or subscribe to *Leadership Insights Online,* contact Top Flight Leadership at www.Top Flight.org or call 866-9LEADER.

  Note: Chapter 1, "Risk, Obedience, and Sacrifice" includes copyrighted material used in this book by permission. You will need to secure separate permission to reprint from the publisher before you can reprint that portion of this book.

- *Subscribe to* Leadership Insights Online. Why not? You get six months for free just for buying this book. We want to come alongside you as you invest in young leaders in the weeks and months to come. Just follow the instructions printed on the inside back cover of this book and start receiving your free subscription. (If for some reason you have problems activating your free subscription, please email info@topflight.org or call 866-9LEADER for assistance.)

  Note: If you received this book for free when you paid for a six-month subscription to *Leadership Insights Online,* the free subscription offer does not apply to you. You got a free book instead!

How were these articles selected and organized?

As this project began to take shape I surveyed the members of my *Leadership Insights* mentoring group, asking them to give me their top ten list of "must include" articles based on what had the most impact on their lives over the past few years. The feedback I received from this group was very helpful in deciding what to include.

We organize our training content at Top Flight Leadership in three "boxes"—spiritual formation, dealing with the character and heart of a young leader; ministry formation, dealing with the gifts and skills of a young leader; and strategic formation, dealing with the values and philosophy of ministry of a young leader. The articles have been loosely arranged in terms of how they fit in each of these boxes. That being said, many of these topics touch on more than one of these boxes and could easily have been listed in a different category. Keep in mind as you read that the topics in each category are not necessarily the most important issues young leaders will face in each of the "three boxes" but merely reflect the content of *Leadership Insights* articles that were included in my email mentoring relationship with young leaders over the past few years.

What leadership discipline has most influenced your thinking?

I admit that this is probably not a question that would have come to your mind as readily as the others addressed in this introduction. But after you start reading these articles, sooner or later you would have begun to wonder about *Leadership Emergence Theory* and the influence of these ideas on my understanding of leadership. So I'm going to beat you to the punch, so to speak, and address the question up front.

My primary leadership mentor is Dr. J. Robert (Bobby) Clinton, Professor of Leadership at the Fuller Theological Seminary School of World Missions. Dr. Clinton has pioneered an approach to leadership known as *Leadership Emergence Theory. Leadership Emergence Theory (LET)* traces the expansion of leadership capacity in a Christian leader over a lifetime. The theory evolved from a comparative study of numerous Christian leaders' analysis of their own lives, analysis of leaders from Church history, and from the Bible.

Many of the articles compiled for this book are sprinkled with *LET* principles. In some cases the entire article is based upon an *LET* idea. Wherever appropriate, footnotes are provided to point you to primary sources of information. If you are interested in an entire book outlining the foundational concepts of *LET* you will probably want to read *The Making of a Leader* by Dr. Clinton, published by NavPress. If you are more inclined to read an article that covers many *LET* principles in a creative story format, I would recommend the chapter entitled "The Lifecycle of a Leader" in the book *Leaders on Leadership*, edited by George Barna and published by Regal Books. Dr. Clinton has authored a number of books expanding on *LET* which are available from Barnabas Resources, 2175 N. Holliston Avenue, Altadena, CA, 91001.

Why is the issue of developing young leaders so important?

I'll admit that if you have purchased this book or taken the time to browse its content long enough for your eyes to fall on this page, I may well be "preaching to the choir." But I can't resist touching on this question because it has been presented to me in one form or another many times over the last few years as I have been giving my entire focus to this life calling. I'll share my answer by recounting a brief story.

In the fall of 1999 I had the privilege of leading an initiative focused on identifying and mobilizing a representative group of young leaders from every region of the world to attend the International Consultation on Discipleship in Eastbourne, England. Dr. Appianda Arthur, who now heads Global Leaders Initiative, organized the event. One of the highlights of the consultation for the young leaders was the opportunity to meet with high-level leaders from around the world in an informal setting where they shared personal experiences from their own leadership journey. At the close of the consultation we assembled the young leaders one last time to give them a final context for what they had just experienced and send them off with a challenge.

Dr. Peter Kuzmic, founder and currently the director of the Evangelical Theological Seminary in Osijek, Croatia, and Professor at Gordon-Conwell

> **God placed the entirety of His plan for the church in the hands of a group of young leaders.**

Theological Seminary, was among several leaders that agreed to share with the young leader delegates. He spoke very openly about key moments in his life as a young leader and how God had strategically guided his early life choices. Then he reminded the group that Jesus himself was by most standards a young leader for his entire earthly ministry, and all of the disciples were in their twenties when Jesus chose them— with the exception of one who was likely still a teenager.

I will never forget the thoughts swirling in my head as Dr. Kuzmic shared with us. God had chosen to place the entirety of His plan for the Church in the hands of a group of young leaders. Talk about a controversial strategy. I'm not sure God could have ever gotten that idea through a committee! God believed that if you want to change the world, gather a group of twentysomething young leaders, pour yourself into them in a highly relational and experiential training model, fill them with the Holy Spirit, and then turn them loose.

Why is training young leaders so important? Because somewhere on the planet, right now, a young leader is dreaming about changing the world. We want to ensure their dreams are God-inspired and come true. Lord, help us invest in young leaders who will change the world again—perhaps one last time!

SPIRITUAL FORMATION

Risk, Sacrifice, and Obedience

> "Too much love is sometimes as bad
> as too much hate."
> —C. T. Studd

"Cannibals want missionaries." In 1908, C. T. Studd read these words on a sign in Liverpool. He had returned to England due to fifteen years of ill health after serving as a missionary in China and India, This clever notice piqued C. T.'s curiosity and drew him into the Liverpool meeting. There he learned from Dr. Karl Kumm about the desperate needs in central Africa. He left the meeting convinced God was calling him to lead one final charge to the inland of Africa and went to a group of businessmen to share his vision. They had offered conditional support—he must first receive medical clearance from the doctors before they would release the funds for this final campaign (he was now 50 years old).

The doctor's report came back unfavorable—if C. T. were to go to Africa he would die. As a result, the businessmen withheld their support. C. T. responded saying, "Too much love is sometimes as bad as too much hate." These men loved him too much to let him risk his life for the cause of Christ. C. T.'s answer to this group of businessmen was straightforward—"Gentlemen, God has called me to go, and I will go. I will blaze the trail, though my grave may only become a stepping stone that younger men may follow."

God raised up the funds from another source, and C. T. Studd did die in Africa—twenty years later, after pioneering a new mission society (Heart of Africa Mission—now known as WEC International). And these businessmen lost a great opportunity to store up more treasure in heaven because they had an inadequate theology of suffering. They were not prepared to allow C. T. Studd to take a God-ordained risk.

Biblical Precedence

The Bible is full of examples of leaders who were called by God to risk everything, including their own lives, for the cause of the Kingdom. Hebrews 11 speaks of others who "were tortured and refused to be released.... Some faced jeers and flogging, while still others were chained and put in prison" (Hebrews 11:35–36). Jesus told the religious leaders of his day, "I am sending you prophets and wise men and teachers. Some of them you will kill and crucify; others you will flog in your synagogues and pursue from town to town" (Matthew 23:34). Paul and Barnabas were described as "men who have risked their lives for the name of our Lord Jesus Christ" (Acts 15:26).

Of course the church in the West looks with great fondness on these heroic examples of faith who were willing to risk suffering for the cause of Christ. We like to tell about the sacrifice of Jim Elliot and his fellow missionaries who died at the hands of indigenous Indians in Ecuador. We are inspired by their example and use stories like this to spruce up our teaching. But very few Western Christian leaders are really prepared to embrace suffering and risk. We live as if God no longer calls His followers to pursue a journey that He knows in advance will involve persecution or even death. We operate with an unspoken arrogance that suggests God used to ask people to lay down their lives but not today—at least not in our hemisphere. People separated from us by time or distance who risked everything for Jesus are labeled heroes. Those up close are labeled fanatics.

The fact of the matter is that God is still calling His followers to a total abandonment and radical discipleship that includes "a chance to die." Amy Carmichael used that phrase to answer a young prospective missionary's question—"What is missionary life like?" Amy responded saying, "Missionary life is a chance to die." It is a chance to die to selfish dreams and human ambitions. A chance to die to fleshly desires and sinful patterns. A chance to offer the ultimate sacrifice—a chance to die.

I believe the Western church is so bankrupt when it comes to a theology of suffering that we are largely incapable of processing risk. Institutionally we are forced by competitive factors to evaluate personal risk in terms of public relations and donor response. Is God still a primary stakeholder in our organizational decision-making grid?

Under what circumstances is it appropriate for Christians to risk suffering and death? Obedience. It's that simple. Paul never went chasing after danger like some sort of Christian Rambo trying to spruce up his resumé or increase his market value with the Christian speaker's bureau. But he refused to shy away from suffering when it was between him and obedience. How else can we process his words in Acts 20:23—"I only know that in every city the Holy Spirit warns me that prison and hardships are facing me." What? Doesn't Paul have it backwards? Shouldn't he be seeking confirmation that he will *not* be imprisoned before agreeing to go? No, actually *we* have it backwards.

What does this have to do with young leaders?

I believe that the Church has saved the hardest and most difficult people groups for last when it comes to finishing the task of world evangelization. The resistant belt of the 10/40 Window (a geographic region from 10 degrees to 40 degrees north of the equator from West Africa to the Pacific Rim) will not be reached without an army of young leaders who are willing to take "a chance to die" in the fullest sense. Without a theology of suffering, the Western church will be reduced to onlookers and bystanders when it comes to the final harvest force.

God is already raising up this kind of radical disciple around the world. I'll never

> ❝ **The resistant belt of the 10/40 Window will not be reached without an army of young leaders who are willing to take a chance to die.** ❞

forget the conversation I had with an Indian young leader who was still recovering from the beating he took from a band of Hindu fanatics. He barely escaped and had witnessed the martyrdom of his partner in ministry. He looked me in the eyes and said, "When I am well I am going back to that village. I will not let my brother's blood be spilt in vain." He was in his early 20's—your typical college student age. He knew that missionary life is a chance to die.

Amy Carmichael raised the issue of suffering and risk in her classic style through the poem entitled *No Scar?* Are you willing to be the kind of leader that is willing to be "scarred" as a price of obedience?

No Scar?

Hast thou no scar?
No hidden scar on foot, or side, or hand?
I hear thee sung as mighty in the land,
I hear them hail thy bright, ascendant star,
Hast thou no scar?

Hast thou no wound?
Yet I was wounded by the archers, spent,
Leaned Me against a tree to die; and rent
By ravening beasts that compassed Me, I swooned;
Hast thou no wound?

No wound? No scar?
Yet, as the Master shall the servant be,
And pierced are the feet that follow me;
But thine are whole; can he have followed far
Who has no wound no scar?

—*Amy Carmichael*

Taken from *Toward Jerusalem* by Amy Carmichael ©The Dohnavur Fellowship, 1936. Published by CLC Publications, Fort Washington, PA. With permission.

WORKING IT OUT

Ideas for Application and Reflection

1. Take a minute to pray for the suffering Church around the world. They are not asking you to pray for an end to the suffering, but for boldness and grace to endure. (Visit the Voice of the Martyrs website at www.persecution.com for more information.)

2. Ask a Christian leader you respect to share their theology of suffering with you. Discuss with him or her your ideas about this issue.

3. Imagine a young leader has come to you for advice regarding a short-term mission trip for which they have been accepted. The mission organization has informed them there is a slight chance they might be arrested or at least detained briefly if they go. What advice would you give them? What would you say to their parents? On what basis should decisions of this nature be made?

4. Read the Amy Carmichael poem *No Scar?* to another leader and discuss what you think she really meant. Do you agree or disagree with her?

Failure and the Next Step

"I said a lot of stupid things... I did not want to go on saying stupid things."

—Winston Churchill

While running for office and on the campaign trail, Winston Churchill encountered a heckler who quoted something Churchill had said while a member of the Conservative Party. He responded, saying, "I said a lot of stupid things when I was with the Conservative Party, and I left them because I did not want to go on saying stupid things."

Churchill had subsequently changed party affiliation and was running as a Liberal for the first time. He was 31 years old. As a young leader Winston Churchill wasn't afraid to admit he was wrong. He had known failure and found it to be a fertile breeding ground for success.

Effective leaders must learn how to deal positively with failure. All leaders fail. Effective leaders face their failures by admitting them quickly, learning the appropriate lessons, and moving forward with confidence. I've been thinking about this important subject, partly due to my study of the life of Winston Churchill. Here is a list of some of Churchill's brushes with failure:

- 1884, age 10—Churchill's school report card reads, "Very bad—is a constant trouble to everyone." Throughout his schooling he achieved very low grades in composition, writing and spelling. Seventy years later he would win the Nobel Prize for Literature.

- 1892, age 17—Churchill failed the Sandhurst entrance examination (equivalent of war college exam) scoring 1300 points below the minimum needed to enter the infantry.

- 1892—The day before his eighteenth birthday, Churchill failed the Sandhurst entrance exam a second time. He said of that time, "It is not pleasant to feel oneself so completely outclassed and left behind at the very beginning of the race." He finally passed on his third and final attempt but was only accepted in the cavalry. This success brought with it the aftertaste of failure—for he had all along been shooting for the infantry.

- 1899, age 24—Churchill lost his first bid for a seat in the House of Commons. He chalked it up as a lesson in communication skills. He had been forced to speak on some evenings three or four times each night. Of this season he said, "I speak now, however, quite easily without preparation, which is a new weapon that will not wear out." He won a seat the next year.

- 1904, age 29—While giving a speech to the House of Commons, Churchill lost his train of thought in mid-sentence. He stopped, appeared confused, and sat down mumbling, "I thank the honorable Members for having listened to me." From that day on he ceased reliance on memorized or spontaneous speeches and would supplement his copious memory with a full manuscript to guide his thoughts.

- 1915, age 40—While serving as First Lord of the Admiralty during World War I, Churchill took the blame for the failure of the campaign in the Dardanelles. He had believed the best way to beat Germans was by launching an attack from the underbelly of Europe through Turkey. The campaign was plagued with inaccurate intelligence and bad luck. He became the scapegoat and was forced out of his position. He wrote in his diary, "I am the victim of political intrigue. I am finished!" Yet within the year he had volunteered to return to the front and was at his post in the trenches of war in the south of France. Once again he would taste the bitterness of war on the edge of the battle, and it would shape his understanding for a future appointment with destiny.

- 1922, age 47—Churchill lost his seat in the General Election while suffering from appendicitis. When the result was declared, Churchill was left, as he wryly observed, without a seat, without a party, and without an appendix.

- 1924, age 49—Having rejoined the Conservatives, Churchill became Chancellor of the Exchequer in Stanley Baldwin's government. Soon he disagreed with party policies, and the Conservatives lost the election of 1929. This put him out of office from 1929 to 1939, although he remained an MP.

- 1945, age 70—Having seen Britain through WWII as Prime Minister, he lost the General Election in 1945. He returned as Prime Minister, winning the election of 1951.

Winston Churchill is a powerful example of how failure in the life of a leader can be turned into a classroom for learning and a platform for future success. In fact, Churchill defined success as "going from failure to failure without loss of enthusiasm." But not all failure is equal. I've identified five specific categories of failure as follows:

- *Failure resulting from the lack of creativity.* Sometimes people fail because they lack the ideas or information needed to get the job done.

- *Failure resulting from the lack of capacity.* Not everyone has the capacity or giftedness to do the job. I will never forget the first time I took a class in college (X-Ray Technology School—Engineering Chemistry) that was beyond my abilities to succeed. I knew no matter how hard I studied I was not going to get an A in that class. I simply did not have the capacity to do so.

- *Failure resulting from the lack of competency.* There is a big difference

> **Churchill definited success as going from failure to failure without loss of enthusiasm.**

between capacity and competency. Sometimes people fail because they have not developed the skill sets needed to get the job done.

- *Failure resulting from the lack of commitment.* Sometimes people fail because they don't do what it takes to get the job done or will not pay the price. This is perhaps the most frustrating type of failure for leaders to accept in those who follow them.

• *Failure resulting from the lack of character.* Sometimes people fail because they crumble from the inside out. The lack of integrity, purity, or personal holiness finally comes to the surface, and no matter how good of a dog and pony show we have going, the circus is over.

Let me say once again—not all failure is equal. All leaders fail and therefore must learn to cultivate honesty followed by resiliency. One of my favorite quotes from my grandfather is this: "Experience is the best teacher but if you can learn any other way, do it." That is especially true of character-based failure. There are some lessons leaders need to understand through the power of vicarious learning.

WORKING IT OUT

Ideas for Application and Reflection

1. When was the last time you experienced a notable failure? (If it has been more than a year you are probably not taking enough risks.) What kind of failure was it (lack of creativity, capacity, competence, commitment, or character)?

2. What lessons did you learn from it? What would you do differently if faced with the same set of circumstances?

3. When was the last time you looked your followers in the face and said one of the following? "I was wrong." "I made a mistake." "I have sinned." Or in the words of Churchill—"I said a lot of stupid things... I left them because I did not want to go on saying stupid things."

4. In what area of your life are you most vulnerable to failure right now? Which of the five categories of failure would most likely trip you up? What steps should you take now to avert failure if at all possible?

Failure and Vicarious Learning

"Failure is the drastic surgery God sometimes has to use to cut the stubborn nerve of self-sufficiency in a leader's life."

—Tom Marshall

There is a fine line between passion, drive, and self-sufficiency. God can't fully use a leader who loses his or her felt need for divine guidance and authority. In the words of Tom Marshall, "Failure is the drastic surgery God sometimes has to use to cut the stubborn nerve of self-sufficiency in a leader's life." This quote comes from the final chapter of the book *Understanding Leadership* entitled "When Leaders Fail." On the one hand, all leaders must learn to deal with failure because we all fail. But when it comes to failure, leaders must embrace vicarious learning for at least two important reasons:

- You don't have enough time to make all the mistakes from which you need to learn.
- The consequences of some types of failure are too costly—especially failure resulting from lack of character.

I came across this example of vicarious learning in the Book of Proverbs:

"I went past the field of the sluggard, past the vineyard of the man who lacks judgment; thorns had come up everywhere, the ground was covered with weeds, and the stone wall was in ruins. I applied my heart to what I observed and learned a lesson from what I saw: A little sleep, a little slumber, a little folding of the hands to rest—and poverty will come on you like a bandit and scarcity like an armed man" (Proverbs 24:30–34).

I couldn't help but notice the phrase, "I applied my heart to what I observed and learned a lesson from what I saw." This is the core principle behind vicarious learning, which empowers us to grow and benefit from the failure of others. I've been trying to apply this principle to the life of Samson. He was a leader who had such an incredible opportunity to influence others and fulfill God's purpose, yet he experienced major character-based failure. My curiosity was piqued regarding Samson, based on his inclusion in Hebrews 11:32 as a role model of the life of faith. While he is among the most infamous of the leaders who surface in the period of the Judges, he is typically known for his failure, not his faith. Here are the fruits of my Samson study.

Background Notes on Samson

Samson is the only military reformer whose selection was revealed by God prior to his conception. This is a unique kind of destiny marker (special birth circumstances) which dramatically emphasizes the purposes of God which will unfold in the life to come. Samson is in rare company on this one— Isaac, Samuel, John the Baptist. No doubt his mother recounted the uniqueness of the angel of the Lord's meeting with her to announce his conception many times.

Samson is the only military reformer given special lifestyle guidance as Nazarite. This, too, spoke of the uniqueness of God's purposes for his life and a daily reminder of being "set apart" for a holy purpose.

There is no biblical evidence Samson had a muscular physique. As a matter of fact, the biblical evidence is just the opposite. If Samson was a muscle-man with arms like legs and legs like tree trunks, why would the Philistines have been so preoccupied with trying to figure out the source of his strength? This was an ordinary man with extraordinary strength. And that drove the Philistines crazy—they had to figure out the source of his superhuman power. And it should have been a powerful reminder to Samson of his felt need for divine strength.

There is uncertainty as to where the events of Judges 16 fit on a timeline. The story of Samson and Delilah is told in Judges 16. But chapter 15 ends with the traditional boundary verse—"Samson led Israel for twenty years in the days of the Philistines." Chapter 16 ends with a similar verse—"He had led Israel twenty years." Some have suggested that the Delilah incident must have happened after Samson's time as the judge over Israel had ended simply because they cannot conceive of an active judge being caught in such blatant sin. The ambiguity of the boundary verses in chapters 15 and 16 complicate the issue.

At the conclusion of the Delilah incident we find one of the most heart-wrenching verses in the Bible—"She called, 'Samson, the Philistines are upon you!' He awoke from his sleep and thought, 'I'll go out as before and shake myself free.' But he did not know that the Lord had left him." Amazing. He did not know that the Lord had left him. The vicarious learner reading this story is naturally faced with this question— how could someone like Samson (prominent destiny markers, marked with a lifelong Nazarite vow, endowed with supernatural strength) arrive at such a place of moral compromise and spiritual dullness? This is a lesson you don't want to learn from experience.

I'd like to suggest five reasons:

Samson settled for the external symbols rather than the inner substance of spiritual vitality. He had the look of a Nazarite without the heart. There is no evidence that Samson ever went beyond the superficial exterior of the Nazarite commitment. In fact, he was everything *but* set apart in his behavior. Far too many leaders make this mistake. They put on a good show, but inside there is no real vitality, no heart reality. Sooner or later the show will come to an end. How are you doing with the little things that feed your spirit and keep you fresh?

Samson believed the defense of his ministry was his responsibility. He personalized the

> **" The fact is that if God built it, He will defend it. "**

attacks against him and became obsessed with revenge—"This time I have a right to get even with the Philistines; I will really harm them.... I won't stop until I get my revenge on you" (chapter 15:3,7). You can learn a lot about what is inside someone when they face opposition. The fact is that if God built it, He will defend it.

Samson believed that effective ministry flowed from personal competency. He became so accustomed to God's Spirit moving upon him with power that he believed this divine channel could be turned on and off like some sort of spiritual faucet. Wrong. It's not about your giftedness or experience, it's about God moving through you. Don't ever take that for granted.

Samson developed an attitude of invincibility. He acted as if he was untouchable, irreplaceable, and unaccountable for his actions. God chose you. But he doesn't need you. Do you get defensive when people criticize you? Do you have regular "in your face" accountability?

Samson chose to remain in a place of vulnerability. Judges 16:16 says, "With such nagging she prodded him day after day until he was tired to death." What a fool. Yet how often do we flirt with temptation on the basis that we're not going to give in? It's ridiculous. There are times when, like Joseph, the only sensible response is to run—even if it means leaving your cloak behind. But Samson chose to stay put, and it cost him dearly.

Praise God this is not the end of Samson's story. In response to God's discipline he:

- *Renewed the spirit of his Nazarite commitment.* Judges 16:22 says, "The hair on his head began to grow again after it had been shaved." You don't need to have a degree in theology to know that hair will grow back after it has been cut. The point behind this verse is not to state the obvious but rather to emphasize Samson's understanding of the significance of not cutting his hair as part of the Nazarite vow. His heart was re-engaged as it relates to the inner reality of this special commitment.

- *Recalled the source of his supernatural strength.* We only have record of two prayers Samson prayed. The first was a selfish request for a drink to quench his thirst, and the second is found in Judges 16:28. It has a completely different feeling to it. Samson is marked by a selflessness and humility that is not seen in his pre-Delilah days. He clearly sees what has been true all along—God is the source of his strength, and he does not have the ability to turn it on and off like a faucet as he pleases.

- *Realized his greatest ministry success.* I believe the reason Samson is listed in Hebrews 11 is because of his final act of triumph over the enemies of God. "He killed many more when he died than while he lived" (Judges 16:30).

Sometimes God has no other choice but to use failure as the drastic surgery to cut the stubborn nerve of self-sufficiency from a leader's life.

This was true of Samson. Let's learn this failure lesson vicariously. I read about a man named Samson. I applied my heart to what I observed and learned a lesson from what I saw. May that be true of each of us.

WORKING IT OUT

Ideas for Application and Reflection

1. Think of someone you personally know who "pulled a Samson." Can you see any similarities in their journey to what can be observed in Samson's life? Take a moment and pray for that person—regardless of where they are now.

2. When was the last time you benefited from vicarious learning? What did you learn and from whom?

3. Share with someone you are mentoring something you have gleaned from the life of Samson, and challenge them to become a vicarious learner.

4. Is there an area of your life where you have become dull to temptation and accustomed to exposing yourself to it? Based on Samson's life, what are the ramifications of ignoring it? What is God asking you to do about it?

David's Last Words, Part 1
Legacy and Godly Leadership

4

"The enduring fascination with epitaphs lies in the momentary glimpse they offer into another person's life."

—Esme Hawes

What would you like to have written on your tombstone? What's interesting about epitaphs is that ordinary people generally write them about ordinary people. They most often carry the sense of endearment and affection felt toward one who was loved and will be missed. But rarely do we have much to say about what will be on our tombstone except through the weight and force of who we were before we died. How will you be remembered?

Perhaps it was this realization that prompted King David to be proactive about formalizing his "last words" in 2 Samuel 23. I use quotes here because we know these were not the last words David spoke before he died, but rather his personal spin on how he wanted to be remembered, the accomplishments of which he was most proud, and the reflective evaluation of what he believed was really important in life.

A Legacy of Intimacy

"These are the last words of David: The oracle of David son of Jesse, 'The oracle of the man exalted by the Most High, the man anointed by the God of Jacob, Israel's singer of songs'" (2 Samuel 23:1).

David begins by acknowledging that he remembers where he came from and how he got to where he was. It is humility and not pride that moves David to highlight that he had been exalted/anointed by God (verse 1). He had no foolish ideas about being a "self-made" man. Hear David's words from earlier in his rule—"'Who am I, O Sovereign Lord, and what is my family, that you have brought me this far?'" (2 Samuel 7:18).

But what I find amazing about the opening refrain in this testimonial Psalm is what David highlights as his final legacy. Try to imagine an elderly King David doing an interview with the Barbara Walters of his day. "David, of all your accomplishments as leader of Israel, for which one do you want to be remembered?" What will he say? Will it be the heroic act of the young leader who killed Goliath? Will it be the visionary foresight of making Jerusalem the capital of the nation and bringing the Ark of the Covenant there? Will it be the administrative skill that turned the nation from a tribal league (which they really were under King Saul) into a well-organized global power?

If this sort of interview was happening today we would be taken to a well-timed commercial break to increase the suspense and provoke some discussion between members of the audience. What do you think David will say?

The commercial is over and we cut back to the interview. David quietly answers, "I want to be remembered as Israel's singer of songs."

What, singer of songs? Did we hear that right? What could he possibly mean by that? Clearly David isn't bragging about his voice. He is not calling our attention to his musical prowess on the harp. Nor is he bragging about his songwriting genius, as if to say, "I knew Psalm 23 was going to be a hit when I wrote it." He is not waving his many "platinum records" in our face. This is not an arrogant or boastful David rhetorically asking, "Don't you wish you were as multitalented as me?" So what is he saying?

I believe David is saying, "I want to be known as the leader who communed intimately with Jehovah through authentic worship." That's how he wants to be remembered. Yes—Israel's singer of songs.

A Proactive Obituary in the Form of Hebrew Poetry

The last words of David are written in the form of Hebrew poetry, just like the Psalms. Hebrew poetry is a way of expressing the relationship between parallel thoughts. Usually this is done through the repetition of phrases in which the members of one phrase relate to the members of another phrase. In layman's terms there are three kinds of parallelisms: same, different, and other. Same parallelisms are used to emphasize a point, different parallelisms reveal a contrast, and other parallelisms expand an idea or introduce a new thought.

With that very basic overview of Hebrew poetry in mind, let's look at the next part of David's last words: "'The Spirit of the Lord spoke through me; his word was on my tongue.... The God of Israel spoke, the Rock of Israel said to me'" (2 Samuel 23:2–3a).

Here we have not just one, but two same parallelisms used to emphatically state that what David is about to say has not originated with him but rather was communicated to him by God. It is a poetic means of adding emphasis to this point. David leans over with his pen and says to all who read—"Hear me, listen carefully, I'm not merely passing along to you some wise counsel that I have accumulated in my years of leadership. What I want to say to you now was very specifically given to me by God." That

> **Godly leadership breeds hope, inspires vision, and fuels opportunities in followers.**

ought to cause all of us to sit up and take notice—especially those of us in leadership positions, because David is about to share what he has learned directly from God about leadership.

God on Godly Leadership

Listen to what God had to say: "When one rules (*Strong's* reference—"have dominion," "have power") over men in righteousness, when he rules in the fear of God, he is like the light of morning at sunrise on a cloudless morning, like the brightness after rain that brings grass from the earth" (2 Samuel 23:3b–4. Note once again the parallelisms.)

The question we need to answer is what was God—through David—trying to say to us about godly leadership through these incredible word pictures written in classic Hebrew poetic form?

I've pondered over this for some time and here are my thoughts:

* *Godly leadership breeds hope, inspires vision, and fuels opportunities in followers.* Listen to this word picture once again—like the light of morning at sunrise on a cloudless morning. Think about the expanse of the horizon as the sun rises on a cloudless day. What does that picture communicate about the impact of a godly leader on his or her followers? To me it is a picture of hope unfolding in the package of a new day. It is the expanse of possibilities, dreams, and visions as

boundless as the horizon. Godly leadership—according to God—has this kind of effect on followers.

- *Godly leadership provides an environment for the growth and development of followers.* It is like the brightness after rain that brings grass from the earth. Think about a time when you stood in an open space after a rain shower with the sun breaking through the clouds. Picture the new growth on the ground or in the trees as the rain is now giving way to the warmth and brightness of the sun. This is—according to God—a picture of godly leadership.

It's almost like David, in this final stage of his leadership, is giving us a reality check from God about our influence over followers. Think of it this way. If your followers were asked to write a poem describing what it is like to serve under your leadership, would they write anything like this? If someone suggested this was a poetic description of what it's like to follow you, would your followers burst out laughing?

I'm not trying to suggest these few lines of Hebrew poetry given to David by God are meant to be the last word on the subject of leadership. Leaders have to make hard choices. Inevitably some followers will bristle under the discipline and focus of godly leaders. Jesus himself said to beware when all men speak well of you. But beyond these understandable exceptions, how do those you are currently leading view your leadership? Are you known by your followers for inspiring hope, vision, and new opportunities? Are you known as a leader who spurs others toward growth, intentionally developing those who follow you? Would God—by these standards—consider you one who rules over men in righteousness and the fear of God?

WORKING IT OUT

Ideas for Application and Reflection

1. If you keep doing what you are right now in terms of personal worship, in fifty years, will you be remembered as someone who knew God intimately—a singer of songs?

2. If one of your followers wanted to experience greater levels of intimacy in worship, would it be a "no-brainer" for them to come to you as a mentor?

3. Write a two or three sentence poem that could be your leadership epitaph. How do you want to be remembered?

4. Ask a sampling of your followers to describe what it's like to be under your leadership using simple word pictures. I dare you.

5

David's Last Words, Part 2
Reflection on the Journey

"At the very least let us see to it that the Devil holds a thanksgiving service in Hell when he gets the news of our departure from the field of the battle."

—C. T. Studd

As leaders move in the direction of "the middle years" they tend to start thinking more about the long-term results of their ministry. In *Leadership Emergence Theory* this lifetime focus is articulated in the form of ultimate contribution statements. For some (probably most) leaders these thoughts are rather fleeting and never coalesce into a focused set of goals.

C. T. Studd powerfully illustrates the tendency of leaders to think about the lifetime results of their ministry with his classic statement, "At the very least let us see to it that the Devil holds a thanksgiving service in Hell when he gets the news of our departure from the field of the battle."

Will the devil even notice when I move into glory? I guess that depends on how my ministry plays out here and now. And that's the paradox. Intentional thinking about the lasting results of my ministry forces me to evaluate what I'm giving myself to today, this week, this month, this year—against the backdrop of my lifetime goals.

In David's last words he, too, spends some time in reflection on his life. Following his comments—as given by God—on godly leadership, David asks three rhetorical questions that I believe summarize what he now sees as important. David is a Core[1] biographical character for me, and I've spent a lot of time studying his life and leadership. I know a lot about David. But I have to confess the ideas I'm about to put forth are hard to prove. I'll let you analyze them for yourself. There won't be much controversy over the validity of the ideas themselves. The question comes when you try to determine if these were the ideas David meant to communicate.

A Lifetime in Reflection

In offering a series of rhetorical questions, David is, in a way, taking a page out of his mentor's book. Samuel, in his farewell speech to Israel, offered his own set of reflective questions. "'I have been your leader from my youth until this day. Here I stand. Testify against me in the presence of the Lord and his anointed. Whose ox have I taken? Whose donkey have I taken? Whom have I cheated? Whom have I oppressed? From whose hand have I accepted a bribe to make me shut my eyes? If I have done any of these, I will make it right'" (1 Samuel 12:2b–3).

The obvious answer to Samuel's questions (as acknowledged by the people) was that he had done none of these things. His leadership through the years was unscathed. There was no stain or blemish. No cloud hanging over his accomplishments. No qualifications needed to be made. They wouldn't have to say, "Other than [fill in the blank], Samuel was a great leader," or "If he only stayed away from [fill in the blank], he would have finished well." Even the little things had been cared for with integrity of heart and hand. Praise God His grace is enough to enable us to overcome failure. But how much better would it be to overcome by not falling in the first place.

So David poses his questions...

- *Is not my house right with God?* (The KJV translates 2 Samuel 23:5 quite differently. Most commentators agree the NIV got it right.)

It's a good thing this is posed as a rhetorical question because David's followers would be hard-pressed to answer him. Clearly David is reach-

---

[1] The idea of Core biographical character comes from Bible Centered Leadership. A Bible Centered Leader, as defined by Dr. J. Robert Clinton in his book *Having Ministry That Lasts,* is one whose leadership is informed by the Bible, has been personally shaped by biblical values, has grasped the intent of scriptural books and their content in such a way as to apply them to current situations, and who uses the Bible in ministry (with power) to impact followers. In the pursuit of lifelong Bible mastery, Bible Centered Leaders identify their Core (loose synonym, *favorite*) material including books, characters, passages, themes, psalms, parables, etc., and develop the skill sets to study Core material in depth.

ing far beyond his own immediate family and embracing the Davidic line established by God's covenant with him. And in this broader sense his house—meaning family—was intact within God's covenant promise. But it is more than ironic to note that David's greatest heritage—the kingly lineage—was mirrored by his greatest failure. No aspect of David's leadership was more wrought with failure than his family.

When David responded to Nathan's parable that set the stage for his confrontation about Bathsheba, David blurted out judgment on the rich man who had taken the ewe lamb from the poor man saying, "He must pay...

> ❝ **I believe David would have traded all the fame and success he achieved in leading Israel for a heathy and wholesome family life.** ❞

four times over" (2 Samuel 12:6). Little did he know he was speaking judgment over himself. Four of David's sons died and his family was torn apart from the inside. (The four who died were the son Bathsheba conceived through their affair; Amnon, killed by Absalom over the rape of his sister; Absalom, killed by Joab during the rebellion against David; and Adonijah, killed under Solomon following the scramble for the throne.)

So what are we to make of David's first rhetorical question? What principle might David have in mind for leaders like us today? *I believe David would say your greatest ministry is your family.* No amount of success can replace the responsibility and priority your family has in the scope of your effective ministry. I believe David would have traded all the fame and success he achieved in leading Israel for a healthy and wholesome family life. Why is it so easy to see this truth when you are old and so hard to see it when the crucial decisions are actually being made?

- *Has he not made an everlasting covenant, arranged and secured in every part?*

In the sovereignty and providence of God a humble shepherd boy has been selected not only to rule Israel but also to provide the lineage of future rulers, culminating in the Messiah. How much of this did David fully understand? We can't say for sure. Jesus spoke of Abraham saying, "'Your father Abraham rejoiced at the thought of seeing my day; he saw it and was glad'" (John 8:56). So who knows for sure what window of revelation David may have received?

While none of us can relate to the specifics of David's words, all of us have our own journey, which God has "arranged and secured in every part." That does not reduce your destiny to fate. The purposes of God in this sense are not automatic. We must choose to cooperate with God in order to fulfill our destiny. But it is not our surrender or obedience that brings destiny fulfillment—it is God, weaving the thread of my life into the tapestry of His everlasting covenant, arranged and secured in every part. What a relief. I don't have to strive, scrape, and claw my way toward destiny fulfillment. I must surrender and obey. I must seize the moment and actively pursue the steps God puts before me. But all this is done against the backdrop of His everlasting covenant. So what is David trying to say to me here? *I believe David is saying your destiny is safe within God's sovereignty.*

- *Will he not bring to fruition my salvation and grant me my every desire?*

Like every leader in a moment of reflection, David acknowledges that his desires or his leadership agenda has not been fully accomplished in his lifetime. This is true for all of us when we see our ministry—even over a lifetime—against the larger backdrop of God's purposes in all of history. My leadership connects like a few pieces of a puzzle with God's greater Kingdom agenda in time and eternity. It is not the colors or shapes of my puzzle pieces that count so much as the picture that forms when all the pieces come together. How much more unity would we see if leaders could actually process this big picture perspective in the heat of the battle?

This tension between a race well run and yet unfinished is heard in Paul's voice when he said he had "fought the good fight... finished the race... kept the faith" (2 Timothy 4:7). Yet he also spoke with passion of his desire to go to Spain and would no doubt have continued on to England had the opportunity been provided. But it was not to be. So what is David trying to tell us? *I believe David is saying your future legacy will be validated in God's final victory.* He will bring to fruition your salvation. And every Kingdom desire will be granted in the consummation of time and eternity.

So David, is there anything else you would like to say before we conclude this interview? Yes. Your greatest ministry is with your family. Your destiny is safe within God's sovereignty. Your future legacy will be validated in God's final victory. Thanks, David, wise words indeed.

WORKING IT OUT

Ideas for Application and Reflection

1. Review the rhetorical questions Samuel asked his followers in his farewell speech. Reflect on the questions David used to frame his life and ministry. Now imagine you are at the end of your life and ministry. You will have two meetings; one with your family, one with all those who have served under your leadership. In a reflective and contemplative moment you list a series of your own "rhetorical questions" that will summarize your relationships, your leadership, and your ministry. What questions do you want to be able to ask?

2. Do you agree or disagree with my conclusions about David's rhetorical questions? If you disagree, what do you think David was trying to say?

3. What have you done this week that would cause the devil to celebrate your departure from the battle?

4. Write your own epitaph. How do you want to be remembered?

David's Mighty Men

6

"Potential leaders are intuitively attracted to
leaders with similar passions,
skills, and gifts."

In the last few articles I've been probing the depths of David's last words
for leadership insights. As I've reflected on what I have learned I asked
myself this question: "What would I think of David if the only thing I
knew about him was his last words?" The more I pondered that question
the more I realized how easy it would be to assume that David was a
wimpy or feel-good sort of leader who lived in an idealistic world somewhat divorced from reality. Think about it—a man who wants to be
known as "Israel's singer of songs." A man who describes effective leadership "like the light of morning at sunrise on a cloudless morning." A man
who sees leadership priorities in issues like family, destiny, and legacy.

For those of us who live and work in down-to earth leadership envi-
ronments it would be easy to think of David's last words as a bit idealistic. How could this kind of leadership produce results in the real world?
How could someone who really led from this paradigm build a quality
team? Doesn't effective leadership require tough, rugged, even hard-
nosed leadership in order to get the job done?

If you find yourself in the mainstream of popular leadership culture
today, you would probably have to admit you relate to these questions,
even if you immediately push them out of your head shortly after they
make themselves known. So rather than dismiss them outright, I want
to take a closer look at David's leadership effectiveness.

Like Attracts Like

Potential leaders are intuitively attracted to leaders with similar passions, skills, and gifts. This dynamic is often referred to as "like attracts like." It is typically associated with a spiritual gifts identification pattern in *Leadership Emergence Theory.* But I believe it extends beyond spiritual gifts to passions and skills. John Maxwell refers to this as the law of magnetism—who you are is who you attract. Of course Maxwell is speaking of overall leadership capacity as much as gifts, skills and passions—10's attract 8's but 6's never attract 9's. (I believe this is true as a general principle but like most generalizations, it breaks down in some cases.)

So based on this principle, what kind of leaders would we expect David to attract? If after reviewing his last words we conclude David's idealism falls short in the real world, we would expect to see him struggle to attract high-level leaders who are ready to sacrifice for the cause and deliver the bottom line—results.

David's Mighty Men

It's convenient that the passage immediately following David's last words is the account of David's mighty men. It chronicles the exploits of David's core followers in the earlier days of his leadership. This passage parallels 1 Chronicles 11. It highlights five of David's warriors individually and then lists thirty-seven others. Here's a quick review of the five:

- *Josheb-Basshebeth*—listed as the chief of the Three, who raised his spear against 800 men, whom he killed in one encounter. Not bad. (The 1 Chronicles passage says 300 and is presumed to be more accurate. Eight hundred or 300, this guy impresses me!)

- *Eleazer*—stood with David after the troops retreated and struck down Philistines till his hand grew tired and "froze to the sword." Probably a cramp that made it difficult to open his clenched fist from the sword. Quite a tough guy.

- *Shammah*—stood alone in the middle of a field defending it against Philistines. The Lord used him to bring about a great victory.

It appears these three men became known as the Three because they broke through enemy lines to get David a drink of water. He was so aghast when he discovered they had risked their lives for him, David poured the water out before the Lord.

- *Abishai*—raised his spear against 300 men and became a leader of the Three, held in greater honor, even though he was not counted among them. (He had not been with them when they went to get water for David.)

- *Benaiah*—known for great exploits including killing two of Moab's best men, a lion, and huge Egyptian. He became the head of David's bodyguards. Could you argue with that choice?

The rest of this chapter lists thirty-seven men who are known as the Thirty. It appears the label "the Thirty" was actually a title or office more than a numerical accounting. The same Hebrew word is used in Exodus 14:7 to describe the captains of Pharaoh's chariots. No specific details are given with regard to the exploits of the Thirty. It is safe to include they were men of courage and bravery with great skill in battle. They were leaders among leaders.

> **David attracted this band of warriors at a time when he had no title, no office, and no organizational power.**

So what does all this say to us about David's leadership? Here are three observations.

- *Intimacy with God, which cultivates a spiritual authority power base, is not incompatible with courage, risk, and bravery.* Keep in mind that many of the psalms were actually written by David during the time he was fleeing from Saul and attracting these courageous followers. These knock-'em-down and drag-'em-out fighters were actually drawn to and respected a man who played the harp and sang love songs to God when he wasn't leading a raiding party. Make no mistake about it—worshiping hard after God is not a sign of weakness. Real men fall on their face before God in worship even when the tough guys are looking.

- *David attracted this band of warriors at a time when he had no title, no office, and no organizational power base.* Most of them came to David when he was in retreat—fleeing for his life from King Saul. When presented with opportunities to show the tough side of his leadership by killing King Saul, David said an emphatic no. (Read

1 Samuel 24 and 26 to refresh your memory.) His character and integrity only enhanced his standing with his men.

• *David had amazing influence over his men—able to enforce his code of ethics and create a godly organizational culture.* Think for example of the final challenge David encountered before learning of Saul's death. It is recorded in 1 Samuel 29 through 30. After being sent away by Achish, David and his men discovered their home base at Ziklag had been burned and their families taken hostage. David rallied his men to pursue the raiding party (an amazing leadership lesson in itself where David motivated a group of men intent on killing him to press through their emotional pain and fatigue to purse their enemies). Some of David's men were too tired to continue the chase and stayed behind. After recovering everything that had been taken from them by the raiding party, some of David's men suggested those who stayed behind should not receive anything from the plunder. David spoke up saying, "'The share of the men who stayed with the supplies is to be the same as that of him who went down to the battle. All will share alike'" (1 Samuel 30:24). This became a statute in Israel under David. What did David have—other than spiritual authority—to enforce this statute? How could he in an instant—single-handedly—issue a leadership edict that was immediately followed? No wimpy leadership here.

To be sure it was David's renown for killing Goliath and his track record in Saul's army that initially attracted this band of soldiers. But his warrior resume did not dominate his leadership style. And he never hid who he really was from them. Yet these tough guys were not repulsed by Israel's singer of songs, or his desire for godly leadership, or his willingness to trust God's sovereignty with his future destiny as king. I guess we shouldn't worry about giving off the wrong signals to our followers by heeding David's last words.

WORKING IT OUT

Ideas for Application and Reflection

1. What leadership behaviors do you most often associate with people who attract high-level leaders as followers? Would vulnerable worship be in your top five?

2. What do you see as being the most important factors that enabled David to lead without a title or position?

3. Think of a situation where you want to have influence but don't have a traditional power base (title or position). What advice might David give you about gaining influence in this context?

4. Have you ever been tempted to hide the more vulnerable and authentic expressions of your pursuit of God for fear you will be misunderstood? According to David, are your concerns valid?

Balanced Christian Leadership

"The essential ingredient of effective Christian leadership is the powerful presence of God.... But if all leaders need is God's power, what's the point of spiritual gifts?"

Christian leaders who aggressively pursue the development of leadership skills often face criticism about their apparent lack of sensitivity to the need for God's power and an over-dependence on leadership principles in the pursuit of effective service. Most leaders have a natural bent toward action with a focus on accomplishing their goals, which can be perceived by followers as a lack of sensitivity to God's leading. Questions like "Where is God in all these plans?" or "Why is there so much emphasis on planning and so little on prayer?" tend to surface in the minds, if not the mouths, of followers.

People walking out this tension between human planning and the power of God often become polarized around two extremes. Leaders are inclined to stereotype followers as hyper-spiritual, hiding behind the cries for more prayer as a basis for embracing the status quo. Followers tend to stereotype leaders as being unspiritual, trying to push a manmade agenda using corporate methodologies, albeit with a thin veneer of spiritual whitewash, in order to sneak their plans past unsuspecting lay leaders. In most cases neither group is entirely correct in their appraisal of the other.

It is true that Christian leaders must have the powerful presence of God active in their lives and ministries in order to be effective. But that is not all leaders need. They also need skills, tools, and spiritual gifts to go along with the power of God in order to accomplish all He asks them to do. The challenge lies in finding the balance between human planning and God's power.

Ezra: A Model of Balanced Leadership

Ezra's life powerfully illustrates the combination of effective leadership skills with the presence of God, resulting in fruitful ministry. Ezra led the second group of exiles from Babylon back to Jerusalem. His ministry followed Zurubbabel and overlapped with Nehemiah, who led the third return from captivity.

As a priest and scribe Ezra was known for studying, obeying, and teaching the law of God (Ezra 7:10). A repeated phrase in the narrative of his life is that "the hand of God" was upon him, referencing the favor, blessing, and power of God that made his leadership effective (Ezra 7:6,9,28; 8:18,22,31). But Ezra also realized the importance of effective leadership skills.

Five Facets of Effective Leadership Modeled by Ezra

The life of this incredibly spiritual priest and scribe is a convincing reminder that leadership initiative and the power of God are not mutually exclusive.

- *Ezra was an effective planner.* Ezra 7:6 says, "The king had granted him [Ezra] everything he asked, for the hand of the Lord his God was on him." We know from this verse that Ezra went to the king and asked for assistance as it related to his mission to return to Jerusalem. Later in the chapter we are given the text of a letter from King Artaxerxes to Ezra, outlining in

> **Ezra's life is a reminder that leadership initiative and the power of God are not mutually exclusive.**

detail what the king gave him. While it is possible that the king gave Ezra some things he did not ask for, we can assume Ezra's wish list is included in this letter. Ezra must have sat down and planned in advance what he was going to need before he asked the king for help. Look at the outline of what the king gave Ezra—his wish list. so to speak.

  —Permission to recruit others, including priests and Levites (verse 13)

  —The king's endorsement of the mission (verse 14)

—Financial resources—silver and gold—from a variety of sources (verses 15–16)

—Decision-making authority over excess funds (verse 18)

—Articles of worship for the temple (verse 19)

—Access to the royal treasury for replacing items in the temple (verse 20)

—Various resources from the treasurers of the Trans-Euphrates (verses 21–22)

—Exemption from all taxes, tributes, and duties for those working in the temple (verse 24)

—Authority to appoint judges and magistrates (verse 25)

—Freedom to teach the law and punish those who disobeyed (verses 25b–26)

This is an amazingly comprehensive wish list that suggests Ezra was a very thorough planner—a trait we rightly associate with effective leadership. But he clearly recognized the need for the "hand of God" to be upon him in order to obtain the favor of the king. Good planning on Ezra's part came together with dependency on the power of God.

- *Ezra was an effective recruiter.* After obtaining in writing the king's support, Ezra "took courage and gathered leading men from Israel" (Ezra 7:28). The first twenty verses of Ezra 8 outline his effectiveness as a mobilizer and recruiter. He had a good sense for the importance of timing and the power of momentum, seizing the opportunity to gather key recruits on the heels of a major victory.

- *Ezra was an effective "delegator."* After assembling the group at the Ahava Canal, Ezra realized they did not have enough Levites on the team. But rather than go himself to continue recruiting, he delegated the task to other leaders. Ezra met with this group, giving them specific instruction as to where to go and what to say. He credited their success once again to "the hand of God" (Ezra 8:18).

- *Ezra was an effective communicator.* Known for his powerful teaching ministry, Ezra was careful to ensure that he explained his message clearly, "so that the people could understand" (Nehemiah 8:8). He was also careful to model what he taught for others, emphasizing personal obedience (Ezra 7:10).

- *Ezra was an effective reformer.* He was willing to face difficult situations head on and pursue a solution even if it would be a challenge to implement. He did not seek to bring about change by wielding organizational power. Instead he drew from the force of his own character and spirituality (Ezra 9).

Planning. Recruitment. Delegation. Communication. Change management. All of these are leadership skills that Ezra brought to the table. Yet they were wonderfully balanced by a sense of dependence on "the hand of God." Effective leaders depend upon the powerful presence of God in their life and ministry. But they also cultivate and utilize a growing set of effective methods and leadership skills. Ezra proves these two expressions of leadership need not be viewed as the opposite ends of a continuum but can be seen as two sides of one coin in the life of a balanced Christian leader.

WORKING IT OUT

Ideas for Application and Reflection

1. If your followers were to rate you on a scale of 1–10 (10 being highest) in terms of your leadership skills or the presence of God's power in your ministry, which do you think they would rate higher? Why? What should you do about it?

2. Think back to a time when you heard followers question leadership based on the lack of a spiritual component in a given plan or project. If Ezra were serving as a consultant to this ministry leader, what advice might he give?

3. There is an old saying that goes something like this: "Pray as if everything depended on God and then work as if everything depended on you." Do you agree or disagree with that statement? Why?

4. Sometimes leaders only let followers see the human side of their plans, reserving the dependency on God component for the "secret prayer closet." What practical steps could you take to ensure followers know about and participate in both sides of this leadership coin?

The Secret Life of a Leader

"Integrity. Think of it this way—who are you when no one else is looking?"

How is your secret life? If you are like me, when you read a question like that you think of those personal and vulnerable moments when you gave in to sin, and amidst the shame of it all you at least can console yourself with the thought that nobody else besides God knows about that proud, angry, or lustful thought. But that is not the secret life I want to deal with here.

Did you realize Jesus very specifically addressed the secret life of the believer? In Matthew 6 Jesus speaks three separate times about the believer's secret life saying, "'Your Father, who sees what is done in secret, will reward you'" (verse 4), "Your Father, who sees what is done in secret, will reward you" (verse 6) and, "Your Father, who sees what is done in secret, will reward you" (verse 18).

What? Rewarded for my secret life? Yes. Of course in this context Jesus is speaking about three specific disciplines of the Christian life:

- giving—"When you give to the needy..." (verse 2)
- praying—"When you pray..." (verse 5)
- fasting—"When you fast..." (verse 16)

So with regard to each of these disciplines Jesus is creating the expectation that these "will" rather than "might" be part of our secret lives.

So I ask you once again—how is your secret life? As a leader you need to set the pace for those who follow you. Even in the secret life. How are you doing?

- *Giving to the needy.* Leadership brings with it a responsibility for raising the funds needed to fulfill the organization's mission. Leaders are usually much better at asking than they are at giving. It is so easy to get caught up in our own ministries and pet projects. When was the last time you anonymously blessed someone in need or some other ministry—above and beyond your local church priorities?

- *Prayer.* None of us pray enough. We all know that the journey as an intercessor will always be uphill. But are you praying regularly for the ministry God has entrusted to you? If you have been called by God to lead a ministry, then you have a responsibility to pray for that ministry.[1] Most leaders intuitively sense this responsibility to pray for their own ministry. But do you regularly pray for the needs of other ministries

> **If you have been called by God to a ministry, then you have a responsibility to pray for that ministry.**

besides your own? Are you giving priority to those personal prayer times that go beyond the meetings you have with your team?

- *Fasting.* Now there is a novel idea. Remember Jesus spoke about all of these using the word *when*, giving the assumption it would be a part of your life. (You all know about the health disclaimers so I won't go there now.) When was the last time you fasted and ratcheted up the intercession level, expressing your spiritual intensity over a given set of needs?

So, my fellow leader, how is your secret life these days? Your Father sees what is done in secret. Is it something for which you will get a reward?

---

[1] In *Leadership Emergence Theory* this is referred to as the Prayer Macro and comes from the life of Samuel, who said, "As for me, far be it from me that I should sin against the Lord by failing to pray for you" (1 Samuel 12:23).

WORKING IT OUT

Ideas for Application and Reflection

1. Do you believe churches or ministries should tithe? If no, why? If yes, to whom?

2. When was the last time you included another church, project, or ministry on the prayer list you develop for a staff or team prayer time? Which organizations should you be praying for?

3. Consider inviting another ministry to come meet with your staff to share specific requests. Take some time to pray over those requests and lay hands on the representative of this ministry.

4. Do some research in the Bible about fasting, or ask a Christian leader you respect to share with you how they approach this "secret" practice. Pick a date and spend it alone with God in prayer and fasting.

MINISTRY
FORMATION

Handling Criticism

Success brings its own set of problems:
"They criticized him sharply."
—Judges 8:1

Leadership is never played out in a relational vacuum. Leaders cannot lead without followers, and sooner or later the interaction between followers as well as between leaders and followers will give rise to conflict. Even in times of success. Take Gideon for example.

Judges 8 is the story of Gideon's victory over the Midianites (and other Eastern peoples) who had been raiding Israel and stealing their crops. With only 300 men and the intervention of God, Gideon managed to put about 135,000 soldiers to flight—120,000 of them killed each other in the confusion. He then moved into the mop-up phase of the battle even though his army was still greatly outnumbered. Gideon had experienced an incredible victory. But success brings its own set of problems.

As soon as the Midianite armies went scrambling for cover, Gideon sent messengers throughout the hill country of Ephraim, rallying additional recruits to help press the battle to the end. An unrecorded number of Ephraimites responded by setting ambushes at strategic positions along the banks of the Jordan River. They captured and beheaded two Midianite kings, Oreb and Zeeb. When they eventually meet up with Gideon "they criticized him sharply." Imagine that.

Gideon had single-handedly rallied Israel against the Midianites and won an amazing victory. He invited the Ephraimites to share in the mop-up campaign, only to face sharp criticism from them for failing to include them in the entire battle. Of course this was a bogus complaint to start with. Gideon had cast a wide net the first time around when he called for the armies to assemble for battle. And although Ephraim is not specifically listed among the tribes from which the recruits came, most scholars agree there were likely Ephraimites in the 22,000 that went home early due to faintheartedness or the nearly 10,000 who lapped water like a dog from the river.

Gideon may well have expected a bit more as a leader, riding on the tidal wave of supernatural success. Most leaders do. But as leaders separate themselves from the pack of followers, they make much better targets for the arrows of criticism. Even in times of great success. Gideon's response was marked by humility and grace, which rather quickly defused the situation. Effective leaders must learn how to handle criticism if they are to respond to failure and build upon success. I have come to believe there are really two phases of responding to criticism as a leader. Phase one is comprised of measures that blunt the force of criticism when it comes, and phase two is focused on how to respond when the heat is on.

Phase One—Curbing Criticism in Advance

Be proactive about helping followers get to know your heart. Be an authentic leader; get real with your followers. Share why as well as what and how. Giving followers a window into your heart will make it easier for them to give you grace when you do something they don't understand or with which they flat-out disagree. When you know someone well you are much better positioned to read between the lines, assume the best, or reserve judgment until you have more information. But some leaders unwittingly set themselves up for criticism by remaining aloof and apart from their followers.

Face failure openly, sharing what you have learned from the experience. Your followers know you aren't perfect so there is no reason to keep up the charade. When you blow it be prepared to admit it—even publicly— when the situation calls for it. Your willingness as a leader to demonstrate this level of trust and honesty with followers takes some of the intrigue out of the "spiritual snipers" in the crowd who are looking for a chance to attack.

Avoid unnecessary surprises. There is an old "Maxwellism" that says "People are down on whatever they are not up on." Give people regular and healthy forums to ask questions and stay in the information loop. Secrecy breeds suspicion. In my role on the executive team of another ministry, I always briefed my staff on the minutes of executive team meetings to which they were not able to attend. I always told the executive team to be careful to emphasize anything they did not want my staff to know about and would routinely push them to answer why when the value of secrecy was not obvious. A great deal of criticism can be avoided when open lines of communication and minimal surprises are hallmarks of the organizational culture.

Navigate change carefully. Even positive change is a potential minefield of criticism. When processing major changes it is always helpful to identify all the stakeholders and give special consideration to those who will be most likely to struggle to embrace the new path.

Phase Two—Under Attack

Refuse to become defensive, even if you have to defend your position. A defensive posture is a surefire way to escalate the criticism to a higher level. The opening moments of a tense standoff are often the most critical. Even when the person leveling the criticism is completely out of line, remember you are the leader and you must accept responsibility to bring calm and grace to bear on the discussion. A favorite opening line for me has often been, "I want you to know that I really value the input of others and want to create an environment where people feel free to share their ideas and feelings with a goal of solving problems and making improve-

> " One of the most important steps to leadership maturity is to separate who you are from what you do. "

ments." That statement alone, combined with a deep breath and gentle pause, can be like dumping a 55-gallon drum of ice water on a flickering match.

Separate your ideas and actions from your identity as a person. One of the most important steps toward leadership maturity you could take to diffuse criticism is to separate who you are as a leader/person from what you think and do. You must consciously choose to give those with whom you serve the prerogative of rejecting your ideas and critiquing your actions without rejecting you. You will never become a high-level leader if everyone you work with needs to take out their "kid gloves" whenever they want to question something you have said or done. I

have found even when I'm processing the criticism it is helpful to ver-
balize my commitment in this area to the person that is sharing with me
by saying, "I want you to know that I am not going assume you are
rejecting me as a person or leader just because you have questions about
what I have said or done. I value my relationship with you and don't
want something like this to undermine our ability to work together pro-
ductively." That kind of maturity from you as a leader beckons followers—even critical ones—to rise to a higher plane in resolving issues.

Give people the benefit of the doubt. I try to make it a discipline whenever
I become aware of a disgruntled person to say to myself, "I'm sure there
is something going on here that I don't know, which if I did, would
make it much easier for me to understand their point of view." I push
myself to begin with the assumption that their motives are good and
deep down they want to solve the problem or improve the situation. Of
course some people just find a sick pleasure in making life miserable for
others. I know of one person who actually told her pastor that she
believed God sent her to the church to remove him from leadership. But
these people aside, when you begin by giving people the benefit of the
doubt and and let them know you are doing so, you can help turn what
began as a fleshly motive into something more constructive.

Assume there is at least a kernel of truth within every criticism. Make it your
goal to find that kernel—or bushel full—and learn from it. This past year
I found myself in one of the most complex leadership challenges of my
life when it comes to dealing with people and processing criticism. In
one of the more heated and tense meetings with the people involved I
was absolutely blindsided by a criticism. One of the women involved said
I was a hard-core chauvinist, completely against women in ministry,
which she believed had caused a great deal of the struggles we were processing. I couldn't believe my ears. No one had even hinted at this
before, and she could not have been farther from the truth about my
theology. For years I have said I believe leadership should be a function
of giftedness and calling and not gender. But all this withstanding, the
criticism was clearly being leveled against me.

I decided to take an inventory on this issue with my closest followers.
Not one of them gave any credence to what had been said. But I decided
there must be a kernel of truth in this and I wanted to learn from it.
So over the next year whenever I found myself relating to women (as

followers or leaders) I proactively sought to conform my actions with my convictions. This simple approach radically altered several very important leadership responsibilities I had that year. To this day I am conscious of the fact that I may unwittingly give off the wrong idea to female followers and work hard to correct this misconception. I owe a debt of gratitude to the woman who had the courage to raise this issue with me.

One of the most significant challenges of leadership is relational conflict. The number three reason why missionaries return from the field before their scheduled furlough is because they can't get along with other missionaries. One major failure in responding to criticism can be enough to completely remove a young leader from the game and fill his or her heart with bitterness for years to come. My prayer is that these principles will help you develop the skills you need to survive this inevitable leadership challenge.

WORKING IT OUT

Ideas for Application and Reflection

1. Think back to the last major criticism you have faced. How, if at all, could applying the ideas in Phase One have helped to diffuse the situation in advance?

2. Who has served as a leadership role model for you when it comes to handling criticism? Which of the ideas in Phase Two do you see in his or her life? What other principles could you glean from the way he or she handles the pressures of criticism?

3. How readily do you separate your actions and ideas from your identity as a person when being criticized? What practical steps could you take to grow in this area?

4. Have you ever been blindsided by the problems that come with success? What could you add to your planning process to prepare for this kind of unintended consequence?

10

Leading in a Crisis

"Leaders are often measured and remembered for how they responded to crisis situations that surfaced on their watch."

One of the hallmarks of effective leadership is the ability to rise to a challenge under pressure. Like the star athlete who wants the ball when the game is on the line, effective leaders are willing to accept responsibility when the organization for which they are responsible is facing a crisis. And how they handle that crisis is critical. In fact, leaders are often measured and remembered for how they respond to crisis situations that surfaced on their watch.

A C-SPAN Survey of Presidential Leadership compared the overall ranking of U.S. presidents with how they ranked in terms of crisis leadership. The top three in the overall ranking—Abraham Lincoln, Franklin Roosevelt, and George Washington—were also the top three in the category of crisis leadership. With few exceptions, the overall ranking of a president's effectiveness was directly connected with how he did in times of crisis. The legacy of a leader is directly related to how that leader responded to crisis.

The Spotlight of Crisis Leadership

Why do followers place such a premium on crisis leadership? Why is so much at stake in terms of a leader's legacy in a season of difficulty? I believe there are three reasons.

- *Followers pay more attention to the actions of their leaders in a time of crisis.* There is a natural desire for leadership in the heart and mind of followers when facing a crisis. This longing for effective leadership causes followers, who at other times appear indifferent to the activity of the leader, to pay attention. They want information. They evaluate the leader's ability to communicate and track the progress of his or her plan with much greater intensity than in a time of stability. The bigger the crisis the brighter the spotlight on the leader.

- *The stakes are much higher in a time of crisis.* Not only are more people paying attention to your leadership in a time of crisis, but most often the downside of failure is—or at least perceived to be—much greater.

- *The results—good or bad—are more obvious in a time of crisis.* Even the most complex crisis situations have a simple bottom line for followers. And they will evaluate the leader against his or her ability to "solve the problem" on their terms. It's much harder for a leader to "spin" the results of a crisis; followers will have an opinion of their own.

Leadership Testing & Crisis Management

A major crisis will test a leader in five important areas, and the results will be visible for all to see.

- *Times of crisis test a leader's ability to check emotions.* Some leadership challenges are very personal and trigger a tidal wave of emotion. Effective leaders are able to rise above the emotion of the moment long enough to gain proper perspective on the situation. This doesn't mean that leaders never display emotion or that they must walk around with a "perpetual game face." Followers want to know that the leader understands them (the "I feel your pain" syndrome) but does not allow emotion to cloud his or her judgment when it comes time to act. Failure to check emotions can predispose a leader to two extremes, denial and revenge. (Of course denial can take on two forms—deny that there is a problem or deny that I had anything to do with it. America will not soon forget the image of Bill Clinton waving his finger at the camera saying, "I did not have sexual relations with that woman.")

- *Times of crisis test a leader's ability to make decisions.* In the face of a crisis everyone asks, "What are we going to do?" It is here that leaders will be reminded of how important it is to have a quality team around them. Often times the process of determining what to do will require input from a variety of disciplines beyond the scope of the leader's direct expertise. And frequently the normal decision-making cycle cannot be followed due to the pressure of time—we need to know now.

- *Times of crisis test a leader's ability to cast vision.* Every leader needs to be able to rally followers around a cause by communicating vision. In practical terms the leader will have to be an effective communicator to get this job done. And the stakes will never be higher. (How many pundits did you hear suggest that President Bush would never give a more important speech than the one he delivered on September 20, 2001, less than two weeks after the terrorist attacks in New York, Pennsylvania, and Washington D.C.?)

- *Times of crisis test a leader's ability to build a coalition.* Factions within an organization as well as partnerships outside may well need to be brought into greater cooperation in order to respond to a crisis. The challenge of building a coalition often depends upon the relationship-building skills and the reputation of the leader in addition to his or her ability to present a clear vision.

- *Times of crisis test a leader's ability to take action.* The bottom line of crisis management is solving problems and getting results. Inevitably that

> **Patience can be important when responding to a crisis. But waiting rarely causes a major problem to go away.**

will include taking some action. Leaders need to understand the importance of timing and develop the ability to "pull the trigger." Patience can be important when responding to a crisis. But waiting, in and of itself, rarely causes a major problem to go away.

It seems obvious but is worth emphasizing that these five crisis management factors build upon each other. The ability to check emotions enables a leader to make better decisions. Making good decisions helps solidify the vision. Casting vision effectively makes building a coalition much easier. Having the coalition in place makes the action you take more effective. And successful actions will likely result in a problem solved or crisis abated.

Whether you like it or not, your legacy as a leader will likely be tied to your ability to deal with crisis situations that surface on your leadership watch. And while you may not be able to predict the crisis, there are some things you can do in advance to increase the chances you will respond effectively.

WORKING IT OUT

Ideas for Application and Reflection

1. Do you agree with the premise that the legacy of a leader will largely be affected by how he or she responds to crises? What has colored your impression of leaders under whom you have served?

2. Think of the last major crisis you faced. Rate yourself on these five factors of crisis leadership. In which category were you highest? In which one were you the lowest?

3. What is the most important proactive step you could take to become a better leader in terms of crisis management? (Feel free to expand beyond the five factors highlighted in this article.)

4. Read 1 Samuel 30 and look for examples in the life of David that relate to the five tests of a leader in a time of crisis. (Hint: Number 3 is there, but no data is given about it. But it must have been one awesome speech to turn this group around and rally them to the cause!)

11

Communicating in a Crisis

"If I had it to do over again, I'd learn
how to communicate."
—Gerald Ford

Effective leaders have the ability to communicate their vision to followers in a compelling manner that gets results. Leaders who do not develop the ability to communicate—both interpersonally and to the group as
a whole—place limits on their effectiveness, all the more so in a time of
crisis.

Having a good strategy and a good spokesperson can help. But like
everything else in leadership, sooner or later the buck stops on the
shoulders of the leader who must be able to "rally the troops" as an
effective communicator. When looking back over his presidency, Gerald
Ford is said to have lamented the fact that he was less than effective as a
communicator, which, more than his skills or ideas, cost him reelection.
He said in response, "If I had to do it over again, I'd learn how to communicate."

General Principles of Crisis Communication

Effective communication, especially in a time of crisis, goes well
beyond being poised behind the podium, having a wide vocabulary, or
having a good speechwriter. While not intended to be an exhaustive list,
here are a few principles to keep in mind.

Prepare in advance. No matter how bizarre or unexpected the circumstances of a crisis may be, followers will tend to look at the leader and
say, "You should have seen that coming." Call it contingency planning,
scenario building, whatever you want—the bottom line is good leaders

anticipate nearly every possible outcome and develop a basic plan of attack as to how they will respond to it.

Sir Ernest Shackleton, the great Antarctic explorer, powerfully modeled this leadership quality. He and his crew were stranded from 1914 to 1916 after their ship *Endurance* was crushed by the ice. Everyone made it home alive, in part

> **The bottom line is good leaders anticipate nearly every possible outcome and develop a plan of attack.**

due to Shackleton's commitment to prepare in advance. Commenting on their situation on the ice flow, Shackleton wrote, "The disaster had been looming ahead for many months, and I had studied my plans for all contingencies a hundred times."

Tell the truth. That seems rather straightforward and universal. And of course it is. But I mention it here because leaders may never be more tempted to stretch the truth than when facing a major crisis, especially if the organization is in some way responsible. I'm sure your lawyer will want to coach you on what not to say so as to minimize your liability, but it is always better to move from a "cover your backside" to a "clear the deck" approach. Sooner or later your followers will find out what really happened, and the lack of trust that results may well be a bigger problem for your leadership than the mistakes that contributed to the crisis.

Hang together. Of course the proverbial alternative is to hang separately. Resist the tendency to look for a scapegoat or a fall guy on whom the crisis can be blamed and then sent packing. I'm not suggesting you shouldn't hold people accountable or make them responsible for their actions. But don't hang them out to dry as a means of saving your own reputation. Few actions build more loyalty in followers than a leader who is willing to take big picture responsibility for organizational issues.

Knowledge is power—so give it away. Ask yourself, "Why would we not share this information with the whole group?" There are numerous reasons why you may choose to limit how widely information is disseminated. But begin with the assumption that we will pass information through the broadest communication corridors available to us unless there is a good reason not to do so. Most leaders operate from just the opposite premise—hold it close to the vest unless you have to share it.

Speak with one voice. Mixed signals quickly erase the confidence of followers. Be sure everyone knows who is authorized to address the issues at hand, and make sure those people are singing the same song. Another reason to tell the truth—it's a lot easier to remember.

What to Say—The Broad Stroke Outline

Probably no leader in the twentieth century more clearly illustrated the importance of effective communication in a time of crisis than Winston Churchill during World War II. As part of a long-term historical mentoring project, I've been reviewing excerpts of Churchill's speeches with the goal of breaking down his overarching communication focus. I've since compared my ideas with the speeches of other leaders in a time of crisis. Here are the three broad-stroke components I believe Churchill—and other leaders—have used effectively to persuade people toward a course of united action.

• *Reality: Persuasion based on logical facts.* Churchill repeatedly made his case with the people of England and the Commonwealth with facts. He wanted to ground their hope in reality not just principle. Following the fall of France to Germany he spoke these words:

> I told the House of Commons… that the worst possibilities were open. I made it perfectly clear that whatever happened in France would make no difference to the resolve of Britain and the British Empire to fight on… if necessary for years, if necessary alone.
> I have thought it right on this occasion to give you some indication of the solid practical grounds upon which we base our inflexible resolve to continue the war. I can assure you that our professional advisors of the three services—very able men—unitedly advise us that we should carry on the war, that we are able to carry on the war, and that there are good and reasonable hopes of final victory.

When the facts were difficult to interpret, Churchill was more than ready to say so, as evidenced in his famous statement about the involvement of Russia in the war:

> I cannot forecast you the action of Russia. It is a riddle, wrapped in a mystery inside an enigma. But perhaps there is a key—that key is Russian national interest.

• *Principle: Persuasion based on lofty ideals.* Churchill went beyond the base level facts and pragmatics of war and addressed the underlying principles that justified the level of commitment and sacrifice he was asking the nation to make. Consider these comments:

> If ever there was a time when men and women who cherish the ideals of the founders of the British and American constitution should take earnest council with one another, that time is now.

Speaking of Finland's stand against Germany…

> If the light of freedom, which burns so brightly in the frozen north, were finally quenched, it might well herald a return to the dark ages when every vestige of human progress during 2000 years would be engulfed.

And referring to the many common people fighting on the front lines…

> This is no war of chieftains or princes, of dynasties or national ambitions. It is a war of peoples and causes… there are vast numbers not only in this island but in every land who will render faithful service in this war whose names will never be known, whose deeds will never be recorded—this is a war of the unknown warrior.

• *History: Persuasion based on the long view of history.* Churchill framed the conflict in which they found themselves against the backdrop of history. He pulled them out of the immediate to a higher plane where they could look with greater perspective on what the stakes really were. It was not just their own freedom or well-being that was on the line. Could the stakes be any higher than this?

> The Battle of Britain is about to begin. Upon this battle depends the survival of Christian civilization… But if we fail, then the whole world, including the United States, including all we have known and cared for will sink into the abyss of a new Dark Age… So let us therefore brace ourselves to our duty and so bear ourselves that if the British Empire and its Commonwealth lasts for a thousand years, men will say this was their finest hour.

Reality. Principle. History. These are the basic tenants of crisis communication as modeled by Churchill, a master of crisis leadership.

WORKING IT OUT

Ideas for Application and Reflection

1. Think back to the last situation you have faced as a leader that could be labeled as a crisis. Which of the five general principles outlined in this article created the biggest challenge for you? How would you navigate this differently if you could do it again?

2. Think of a worst-case scenario that could occur in your sphere of influence. How prepared are you to respond from a communication vantage point?

3. Thankfully, not every crisis fits in the "finest hour" category. How can the long view of history be of help to you as a leader when evaluating a crisis of lesser proportions?

4. Spend a few minutes praying for a leader you know who is facing a crisis situation. What in this article could you share with him or her as a source of inspiration and encouragement?

5. Review the text of a major speech (such as President Bush's on September 20, 2001, responding to the September 11 attacks on America), and listen for the combination of reality, principle, and history. Are all of these present?

Intentional Modeling

**"Preach the gospel at all times.
If necessary, use words."**
—Saint Francis of Assisi

The weight and force of a godly life can hardly be measured. And people are looking even when you think you are anonymous. As a young leader one of my mentors shared with me about a seminar he had just attended. On the way to the seminar there was a problem with weather and a number of flights were canceled. My mentor found himself at a connecting city with many other frustrated travelers vying for a few prized seats on remaining flights. One elderly man made a huge scene at the gate, humiliating and berating the gate agent. My mentor felt so bad for the gate agent he volunteered to give up his seat for this frustrated traveler even though he knew he might not make it to the conference on time. After arriving at the conference the nationally known speaker for the event introduced the audience to his father, calling him to the platform. He explained that much of what he was sharing that weekend he had learned from the modeling of his father. My mentor was shocked to discover the ministry leader's father was the same man who made the scene at the airport the day before. Modeling is a two-edged sword.

Modeling is an important part of effective leadership. I believe effective leaders proactively use modeling to introduce and reinforce values and skills to followers. The apostle Paul used modeling as a priority leadership development method more than anyone in the Bible. Consider the following examples:

- "I urge you to imitate me. For this reason I am sending to you Timothy my son, whom I love, who is faithful in the Lord. He will remind you of my way of life in Christ Jesus, which agrees with what I teach everywhere in every church" (1 Corinthians 4:16–17).

- "Follow my example, as I follow the example of Christ" (1 Corinthians 11:1).

- "Join with others in following my example, brothers, and take note of those who live according to the pattern we gave you" (Philippians 3:17).

- "Whatever you have learned or received or heard from me, or seen in me—put it into practice" (Philippians 4:9).

- "You, however, know all about my teaching, my way of life, my purpose, faith, patience, love, endurance, persecutions, sufferings— what kinds of things happened to me in Antioch, Iconium and Lystra, the persecutions I endured" (2 Timothy 3:10–11).

It would be a classic understatement to say Paul was proactive about modeling. Paul viewed modeling as a priority leadership and ministry method—not merely a byproduct of the increased visibility that often comes with leadership. Paul encouraged his two primary mentees to use modeling as well—"Set an example for the believers" (1 Timothy 4:12), and "In everything set them an example" (Titus 2:7).

So I have been wondering how to use modeling more intentionally as a leader. Here are six principles that I believe will help you use this powerful leadership development tool more effectively.

- *Take on the mantle of a role model—use intentional modeling as a method for developing people.* This is a sobering step but one that will serve to press you to depend upon God and stretch to reach your full potential. When was the last time you encouraged someone to watch what you do in a specific area and imitate you?

- *Identify the people over whom you have influence as a model.* Think specifically about what you want to model for them and how you will do it. For example, I have identified my children, interns that work with me, active mentees, and people God brings into my life through public ministry as people for whom I want to become a proactive role model. I am seeking to identify specific issues I want to communicate via modeling for each group. For example, I want to be a model for my kids, and I'm trying to be intentional about doing so. One of the reasons I open the door for my wife every time we get in the car is because I have three daughters, and I want to create expectations for them about how a husband treats a wife. I often bring a rose home from speaking trips for the same reason. Do you know your targets and what you want to communicate to them by way of modeling?

- *Get up close to some of the people you are leading in a vulnerable, authentic relationship.* How can you fully utilize the power of modeling if your life is removed from the people you want to influence? No doubt this is why Jesus wanted the disciples to be "with him" (Mark 3:14). How else could Paul be sure Timothy knew his way of life and purpose except that they had an up-close and personal relationship.

> " **How can you fully utilize the power of modeling if your life is removed from the people you want to influence?** "

How often do you speak openly about what God is teaching you, your failures, and your prayer closet experiences?

- *Explain the "why" behind the "what" of your actions.* Model values and principles in addition to behavior. If you have ever been around a leader who makes a decision and then stops to explain how that decision fits within his or her philosophy of ministry or core values you know how powerful this act can be. Of course you must have a sense for how to make decisions in a manner that flows from your values and ministry philosophy in order to model it for others. Do you have a cohesive philosophy of ministry and core values?

- *Identify, develop, and share openly the transferable principles connected with your priority skill sets.* I regularly seek to model a focused life (one that is purposefully organized around my understanding of my life mission, effective methods, major role, and ultimate contribution statements), a Bible-centered ministry, proactive personal growth, intimate worship, and a passion for frontier missions. In what areas have you developed high levels of passion and competence? Do you talk about these in ways that will cause others to want to learn about them?

- *Live what you believe over time with consistency.* That sounds automatic. But the culture in which we live today (especially here in the West) demands authenticity. People are asking the pragmatic question "Does it work?" Your life, more than your words, will be the answer to that question. When you mess up, admit it quickly and move on. I believe the reason Paul could say, "Imitate me" with such confidence is not because he was perfect but because one of his standard practices was to admit when he was wrong and ask forgiveness.

Of course there is another side to modeling. You can't install a filter that only allows the positive aspects of your life to be transferred to others. I saw a cartoon that had a woman speaking to her friend saying, "In spite of my efforts to teach our children good manners and personal responsibility, they still imitate their father." God help me to be a model worthy of imitation.

WORKING IT OUT

Ideas for Application and Reflection

1. Identify the people or groups with whom you should be utilizing intentional modeling.

2. Identify the key issues you want to model for each person or group.

3. Assess the level of relationship you have with the people you identified in question 1. Do you relate to them in a vulnerable and authentic manner? Are you close enough to model intentionally?

4. Think of an area where you excel. How readily transferable are the principles that make you effective in this area? How could you model this value, skill, or behavior on purpose for others?

13

Historical Mentoring

**"If you want to be a great leader, hang around
with great leaders."**

—Unknown

It has often been said that more is caught than taught. Perhaps that is
why Jesus called the disciples so "that they might be with him" (Mark
3:14). If you associate with the right people you will have opportunity to
glean powerful principles from their lives through modeling and formal
teaching. I love to get alongside great leaders and intentionally seek to
maximize the opportunity to learn from them.

Some time ago I had the chance to have breakfast with Tom Phillips,
who at the time was the president of International Students, Inc. Tom
served for twenty years with the Billy Graham Evangelistic Association
and has now returned to their team, serving as Director of Training for
the Cove. He has a wealth of knowledge and experience. I spent about
an hour preparing for my meeting with him by writing down the areas
of expertise I know Tom has and then the questions I wanted to ask him
about each area. Our meeting was very fast moving as we went from
item to item. I filled up several pages of a yellow pad with notes and
quotes. I took one of my interns with me and allowed him to ask a few
questions of his own. I have reviewed my notes several times since our
meeting seeking to glean the most I can from it. Why? Because if you
want to be a great leader, you should hang around with great leaders.

I'm sure there is nothing new here for most of us. But what about the
person who feels like there aren't any (or enough) great leaders around
to hang out with? I have asked that question myself at times. It is part of
what sparked my personal passion for historical mentoring. I have come

to believe that through the biographies of great leaders I can hang around with great leaders. It is amazing to me how few people I meet actually read biographies. Just as mind-boggling for me is how little those who do read them seem to get out of the experience. Over and over again I have met people who say, "Yeah, I read the life of Hudson Taylor" (or fill in the blank—it doesn't really matter who the historical mentor is). But when I ask a simple follow-up question like "What was the most important principle you learned from his life and from what experience did that lesson arise?" I am greeted by a blank stare. I usually take them off the hook by sharing my favorite lesson(s) and what from his or her life sparked it. By the time I'm finished they forget about my question and hopefully move on with a renewed passion to reread the biography with a goal of being mentored.

That's really the bottom line here—historical *mentoring*. I read biographies with the goal of being mentored by the person about whom I'm reading. Last year I was mentored by D. L. Moody and J. O. Fraser (a China Inland missionary to southwest China). You can imagine what kind of look I get when I am asked who my mentors are and I include people like that in my current list! But it's true. This year I'm going to be mentored by Winston Churchill. And I can't wait to get started meeting with him. He will never be too busy to meet with me. Every meeting will happen on my schedule—whether I'm on a plane or in a hotel room or just in my office a few hours early.

How to Benefit From Biographies

Maintain a perspective as to where the mentor fits in history. Disassociating historical mentors from their place in history robs us of an important sense of perspective. Questions about the sociopolitical climate of a historical mentor's world need to be answered in order for us to meaningfully process the events of their life. It usually helps to construct a basic timeline and develop the historical setting out of which the timeline arises. This will allow you to evaluate the impact history had on the individual as well as the individual's impact on history.

For example, Samuel Mill's mother offered him to God for missionary service as a young boy. This is a noble act of faith in any generation. But when she did it, there were no North American mission agencies, and no one from this continent had gone out as a missionary! No wonder the idea stuck in young Samuel's mind..He eventually did play an important role in the formation of the first North American mission board along with the sending of America's first missionaries!

Read with a sense of purpose—know what you are looking for. Seek to identify process items in each stage of the historical mentor's timeline. Process items include the ways and means used by God to move a person along toward leadership. They may be events, people, circumstances, interventions, and inner life lessons. (If you want to learn more about processing and leadership development, read *The Making of a Leader* by Robert Clinton. *Leadership Emergence Theory* has identified about fifty-three different kinds of process items.) Look for clues to the historical mentor's leadership style, how they managed change, dealt with failure or opposition. Make note of their most effective methods. How did they refine them? Where they innovators, reformers, or pioneers? Did they make extraordinary sacrifices or face difficult suffering?

Become a member of the historical mentor's inner circle. Most great leaders get close to only a handful of people. The higher up the leadership ladder they climb, the more inaccessible they become to the broad base of their constituency. But through a biography, you can literally move into the inner circle of leaders who surrounded a historical mentor. You can sit in on board meetings, read personal letters—even journal entries! Pay attention to those inner circle moments as you read.

Identify the important windows of opportunity in the historical mentor's life. In the devel-

> **Through a biography you can move into the inner circle of leaders who surrounded a historical mentor.**

opmental stages of most leaders, there are a few key windows of opportunity through which the primary focus of their ministry is opened. Much can be learned from identifying and evaluating those key moments. How did God prepare the mentor for these opportunities? How long did they get ready? Did they have a sense of destiny regarding their ministry focus? How rapidly did their ministry unfold after the windows of opportunity were opened? What were the key factors in their decision to take new steps of faith? Were these crisis moments of decision, or did they unfold over time?

Identify the historical mentor's ultimate contribution. An ultimate contribution is defined as a lasting legacy of Christian workers for which they are remembered and which furthers the cause of Christianity by one or more of the following: setting standards for life and ministry; impacting lives by enfolding them into God's kingdom or developing them once in the Kingdom; serving as a stimulus for change, leaving behind an organization, institution, or movement that serves as a channel through which God can work; or the discovery or promotion of ideas and communication that furthers God's work.

When evaluating the lives of historical mentors, there are scores of potential categories for ultimate contributions. The thrust of these can be a model life, a model ministry style, productive ministry with individuals, productive ministry with large groups, righting wrongs in society, creative breakthroughs, new organizations, new ideas, well-received written material, mobilization of people or disseminating ideas, and pioneering new fields.

Keep a quote on file that summarizes a main principle you have gleaned from the historical mentor. I have found quotes and vignettes or short narrative stories to be powerful means for remembering the valuable lessons gleaned from a mentoring relationship with a great leader from history.

I mentioned earlier that I will begin a mentoring relationship with Winston Churchill in a few weeks. I plan to read a biography, read a book on his communication style, read a topically organized book on major themes of his life, and listen to audiotapes of his major speeches. This summer I'm going to be in London and will use a portion of my free time to check out the Churchill sites. Imagine that. One of the world's most incredible leaders who emerged at a strategic moment in history is going to mentor me. What a privilege. Who's mentoring you this year?

Note: A major portion of this chapter, written by Steve Moore, was originally published in the book *It's My Turn: How You Can Be Mentored by Christianity's Greatest Leaders,* published by Kingdom Building Ministries (www.KBM.org) and is used by permission.

WORKING IT OUT

Ideas for Application and Reflection

1. Have you ever really had a historical mentor or just read biographies? Consider digging out a favorite biography and enlisting a new mentor.

2. Read a book that profiles a number of historical mentors, such as *They Found the Secret* or *It's My Turn*. Select a new mentor for additional study.

3. After choosing a new historical mentor, imagine you were going to spend a weekend on retreat together. Based on what you know about this mentor, make a list of questions you would want to ask him or her. Write these questions in the front of the biography, and as you read, note the page numbers of any information you find in the book that speaks to each question.

4. Take some time after working through the book to prepare a summary page of what you learned from this mentor. Be intentional about sharing your favorite quote or story with a friend to reinforce what you have learned and to stimulate others to pursue historical mentoring.

14

Lessons on Communication
From D. L. Moody

"We have got to sink self... What for? That no flesh may glory in His sight."

—D. L. Moody

Dwight Moody had a powerful platform ministry. Yet he recognized how easily the lure of the crowd could spoil the heart of a communicator. Speaking on his attitude towards public ministry, Moody said, "We have got to sink self... We have got to get rid of this man worship before [we see] deep work. We want the great, the mighty, but God takes the foolish things, the despised things, the things which are not. What for? That no flesh may glory in His sight." He went on to say that if we "say we have got such great meetings and such great crowds are coming, and get to thinking about crowds and about the people, and get our minds off from God, and are not constantly in communion with Him, lifting our hearts in prayer, this work will be a stupendous failure."

Moody has been a valuable mentor to me. When I began to pursue him as a historical mentor I asked myself what I might want him to focus on if he could spend a weekend with me on retreat. I decided that Moody would be a powerful coach in effective communication. It is amazing how powerfully God used this man who had no formal training (although a profound study habit and learning posture) or education in public ministry. Motivated to learn from Moody the communicator, I found a good biography on his life, *A Passion for Souls* by Lyle W. Dorsett, and got started. Here are the principles he shared with me.

Be sensitive to the length of the message. Moody could hold an audience for a long time with his passion, wit, and powerful delivery. But he was always sensitive to the size of the audience, the conditions of the building and the length of the preliminaries. One woman who heard him preach many times noted that he would often cut his talk to 25–30 minutes if the occasion called for it.

As a guest speaker I am often confronted with the fact that although promised 45 minutes by the organizers (who are whispering "take as long as you need on the platform") the audience clearly would prefer 25 minutes. Sensitivity to the audience and the occasion is something Mr. Moody emphasized to me.

Preach for a specific decision. Moody always had a goal in mind when he stood up to speak. Most of the time it was salvation since he was an evangelist, but he also spoke about world missions and the need to be filled with the Holy Spirit. It was said of Moody by a contemporary, "He aims at one thing... and he brings everything to bear on the one object... From his aim he is never for a moment diverted." Moody challenged me to ask myself, "What is the most important decision I am asking my hearers to make?"

> ❝ **The more we learn and study, the more tempted we are to complicate rather than simplify truth.** ❞

Keep it simple—focus on the common man. A. T. Pierson, a seminary professor who worked closely with Moody in his mobilization of students for missions said of him, "He had learned to preach simply—let us rather say he had not learned to preach otherwise; and in the unaffected language of nature, uncorrupted by the fastidious culture of the schools, he spoke face to face with men; and they heard him." (Only a seminary professor could use such language to describe an unlearned preacher!)

The more we learn and study, the more tempted we are to complicate rather than simplify truth. As my grandmother would say, "Good preachers put the cookies on the bottom shelf." Moody modeled a style of communication that was "earthy" and yet "heavenly" at the same time.

Speak about relevant topics. Moody was very interested in the felt needs of people. He wanted to speak to them where they were and address the concerns on their hearts. Moody used a special meeting called the question-drawer. These meetings began with prayer and then all attendees were encouraged to write one question on a sheet of paper and place it in a box that would be passed around the room. Moody would assemble some keen pastors from the local area to join with him in responding to questions one at a time as they were pulled from the box. He insisted the meetings start and end on time—one hour in length. The pastors would always answer first (which Moody used as a time of learning for himself from those who had formal training). Moody listened carefully to what people were asking and selected sermons as well as illustrations that related to the themes emerging from the questions.

Moody exhorted me to ask myself if anyone in my audience really cares about the topic at hand. Does this speak to an issue they are facing? The more relevant my topics, the better I will connect with the audience. Keeping in touch with the people in my audience will require creativity. How can I recreate Moody's question-drawer?

Illustrate principles with stories. Moody was a master storyteller. He captured the hearts of his listeners by weaving down-to-earth stories into his messages. Even simple Bible stories came to life as Moody's imagination connected with familiar truth. Listeners felt at home with Moody and saw themselves in his message. Moody would fit right in with postmoderns who love stories and receive truth far more readily in narratives than outlines.

Add creativity and spontaneity to preparation. Moody was not formally educated for ministry, but he was a highly disciplined learner. He prepared carefully for his preaching assignments. But he never allowed preparation to undermine creativity and spirit sensitivity on the platform. A unique example of Moody's creativity came in his ministry to children where in one city he unveiled a "wordless book" with four leaves—black, red, white, and gold. With this visual aid he engaged the children with a combination of questions and illustrations focused on explaining the message of salvation. This simple tool caught on in the U.K. and eventually here in the United States, albeit in modified form.

Moody's spontaneity was as unconventional as it was uncanny. One notable example came in a meeting in England where he found himself on the platform listening to a minister drone on in prayer. Moody jumped to his feet and shouted to the audience, "Let us sing a hymn while our brother finishes his prayer." Standing in the back that night was a young medical student by the name of Wilfred Grenfell. He had wandered into the meeting on his way home from visiting some hospital patients. He stood there listening to the prayer for a few moments and was on his way out just as Moody jumped to his feet. Grenfell had never been exposed to this spiritual common sense and unconventionality. He decided to stay. Grenfell was captivated by Moody's message. He took a booklet on his way out and began reading the Bible. He eventually surrendered to Christ, turned his back on a life of privilege in England and went to Labrador as a medical missionary. He gave his life in service to the long-neglected population of Indians, Eskimos, and whites. Late in his life, upon receiving numerous honors for his long-term service, Grenfell credited Moody as the man God used to turn his heart to Christ and steer him toward missions. Moody's example pushes me to listen carefully to those inner promptings of the Holy Spirit—even the unconventional ones.

Anchor your teaching in the Word of God. Moody was clearly a man of one Book. R. A. Torrey said God used Moody because he was "a deep and practical student of the Bible." Moody emphasized to Torrey his need to study the Bible daily and apply the truth of the Word to daily life. In order to do that Moody said "I have got to get up before the other folks get up." Once Torrey spent the night at Moody's Northfield residence. He awoke at 5:00 A.M. to Moody's voice calling, "Torrey, are you up?" He happened to be awake, and Moody asked him to come downstairs because he wanted to show him something. Torrey discovered Moody had been up for several hours in his room studying the Scriptures. At his Mount Hermon and Northfield training centers he made the study of the English Bible a priority. Moody believed the Bible illuminated the study of every other subject. Moody challenged me to remain disciplined and committed to the study of God's Word, using it as the anchor point for all of my public ministry.

Stay focused on individuals rather than crowds. After a decade of preaching Moody purposefully reevaluated his ministry strategy. He became convinced of the importance of a personal ministry. Truly effective work was done after the meeting in his inquiry rooms where laymen (often trained by Moody) met individually with seekers. Moody once taught about the need for personal work at a convention saying, "People are not usually converted under the preaching of a minister. It is in the inquiry meeting that they are most likely to be brought to Christ." He believed Jesus carried on an individual ministry, customizing his interaction with the needs and background of people. He believed "we must have personal work—hand-to-hand work—if we are to have results."

Moody had himself been profoundly impacted by personal ministry. He never forgot the influence of a teacher at Northfield and a Sunday school teacher in Boston. When working with college students Moody took time with them individually, looking them in the eyes, placing a hand on their shoulder, and offering personal words of hope. It was this side of Moody that most of the people who knew him remembered. Moody challenged me to ask God to help me find the "less people" in each crowd with whom I need to spend more time in order to bring about greater Kingdom impact.

It has been a stretching experience to be mentored by Moody in the area of communication. I'm still working on much of what he taught me. And as you can see, there is a big difference between reading a biography and having a historical mentor. Are you hungry to grow in a specific area but struggling to find a mentor? Take another look in that "crowd of witnesses" and you will be surprised to discover some of the greatest leaders in the history of the church are sitting on the shelf of a library or bookstore near you just waiting for your invitation.

WORKING IT OUT

Ideas for Application and Reflection

1. Leadership almost always includes some measure of communication. In what ways might Moody challenge you to grow as a communicator?

2. Ask someone who knows you well to read this article. Then ask him or her to share which of Moody's communication ideas you most need to apply.

3. Develop a short teaching or full-blown seminar on effective communication—Moody style—and share it with some other leaders.

4. Observe some effective communicators and look for how much of Mr. Moody's ideas you can see in their speaking. Do they reinforce his ideas or expand upon them? Interview one of the leaders you observe, using this article as a launching pad for your discussion.

15

Leadership Selection

"There is a treasure, if you can only find it, in the heart of every man."

—Winston Churchill

Winston Churchill was a master change-agent. Wherever he served in government (in very diverse roles) he quickly assessed the situation and developed an ambitious agenda for change. As Home Secretary he led major reform with regard to police and prisoners. This included recreation, entertainment, and education for the prison population. He wanted them to have every opportunity to better themselves while paying for their crimes. His motives were buried in this statement: "There is a treasure, if you can only find it, in the heart of every man." Churchill believed that prisoners should not be written off and that efforts must be made to go beyond punitive to redemptive measures in dealing with them.

Of course as Christians, we believe the treasure in the heart of every man is the image of God in which we were created. It flows from that to a life that has intrinsic value simply because a person exists—not because of what they do. But I believe there is an important lesson related to leadership selection in this statement.

I agree with the principle that says effective leaders view the selection and development of other leaders as a primary responsibility. Every movement is only one generation of leaders removed from extinction. And it is the responsibility of the present leaders to ensure there are quality future leaders.

Mining for Leadership Treasure

As leaders pursue the development of future leaders they must begin by selecting those worthy of investment. When you are dealing with young leaders, finding the leadership treasure (which of course is not in every man) can be challenging. One of the most common criticisms of contemporary leadership models is that leadership selection has been reduced to some sort of popularity contest. You skim the cream off the top of the milk by taking the young leaders who are likeable, outgoing, and popular—ignoring everyone else, and in doing so, missing some buried leadership treasure worthy of being mined.

I'm not just speaking hypothetically here. Several of us at Top Flight Leadership have been approached by leaders of other ministries accusing us of this style of leadership selection. In some cases it was a gentle exhortation, in others it was a bit more confrontational.

This is where Churchill's statement helps me. I really do believe there is a treasure in the heart of every man and woman. In some cases that treasure chest of God's imprint includes leadership; in some cases it doesn't. And it is

> **The quiet kid in the corner may well be the best future leader in the group.**

easy to fall into the trap of superficial mining practices and miss some valuable nuggets. So what's the key to this process? I'd like to give you a few simple cautions when it comes to mining for leadership treasure—especially with younger leaders.

- *Be careful not to mislabel personality as leadership giftedness.* We all know that leaders come in all personality types. So don't let the people who aren't so easily noticed slip through your mining pan. The quiet kid in the corner may well be best future leader in the group.

- *Be careful not to mislabel persistence as stubbornness.* The young leader who keeps doing the same stupid thing over and over again may just be demonstrating a misguided persistence that will serve him or her well later on. It's easy to brand someone as foolhardy or stubborn when really the treasure inside is a persistence that won't give in so easily when the going gets tough. (Take Peter, for example.)

- *Be careful not to mislabel problem solving as rebellion.* The person who always challenges the idea, always asks why, always wants to push for another option, may not be in need of a smack on the side of the head. (Of course some of them need two.) It may be what you are seeing is the very beginning trace of a deep vein of problem-solving leadership treasure that is hiding underneath a pile of immature dirt and rock. If so, be willing to get out your pickax and shovel. Then dig.

- *Be careful not to mislabel adventure or risk taking as fringe behavior.* There is a difference between a serious "notice me, acknowledge me" syndrome and a natural bent to be different, try new things, and take risks. Sometimes real leadership potential is overlooked because people are branded as freaks on the fringe and never really given a chance to blaze the right kind of trail.

- *Be careful not to mislabel honest filtering as erratic behavior.* One of the common threads for young leaders is an instinctive desire to test the motives of those who show an interest in developing them. They often have suspicion of organizational leadership and can stereotype you as someone with a hidden agenda. The problem is the way they go about filtering your motives may well include using an expletive in conversation or sharing a sin pattern that you may have struggled with but won't even confess out loud to God. Give them your best Mount Rushmore imitation and move on. You'll have time to work on their issues later.

Clearly this is not an exhaustive list but I think you can begin to see how important it is to dig beneath the surface when developing young leaders. Become a miner of leadership treasure.

Jesus, the Master Miner

Jesus modeled a willingness to get beyond the surface in selecting leaders. Some of those who attack the emphasis on developing leaders suggest the disciples were not leaders at all. I reject that assertion out of hand. They were effective leaders—but some of them had rough edges that may have obscured the leadership treasure for those unwilling to get their hands dirty as a miner of human potential and divine destiny. Thankfully, Jesus wasn't so easily misled.

WORKING IT OUT

Ideas for Application and Reflection

1. Can you think of someone you may have overlooked for leadership because of one of the mentioned issues or some related concern? Is it too late to do something about it?

2. What can you learn from this experience?

3. Were you ever misunderstood because of one of the issues raised in this article? How did you overcome it? How could that experience form your efforts to develop young leaders?

4. Have you ever seen personality at either extreme (outgoing or introverted) confuse the issue of leadership potential? How could you overcome this common mistake?

16

Reading Right:
How to Get the Most From a Book

"Leadership development is synonymous with personal development."

—Henry Blackaby

Effective leaders maintain an aptitude for learning throughout all of life. Show me a great leader, and I'll show you a hungry learner. The old Irish proverb is true: "You have to do your own growing, no matter how tall your grandfather is." When a leader grows, he or she opens the door to organizational growth. In the words of Henry Blackaby, "As leaders grow personally, they increase their capacity to lead. As they increase their capacity to lead, they enlarge the capacity of their organization to grow. Therefore, the best thing leaders can do for their organization is to grow personally."

One of the most basic expressions of a desire for growth and openness to learn is a leader who is a disciplined reader. Read any good books lately?

I routinely ask that question of leaders around the world as I interact with them. I find many of the books I read have been recommended to me by people I respect. But in asking this question—Have you read any good books lately?—I have learned that not all leaders are readers and that not all readers are learners. Let me explain.

Sometimes when I ask a leader what he or she has been reading I'm met with a blank stare—that "deer in the headlights" look that makes me feel as awkward for a moment as they do. I usually try to bail them out by recommending a book I'm reading or one I feel could be helpful based on where they are in their journey. I want to gently nudge this kind of leader to become a reader because I know they will be vulnerable to "plateauing" if they don't cultivate the discipline of personal growth. One of the most common barriers to finishing well is to plateau as a leader.

Other times I find leaders are quick to list the latest books they have purchased and begun to read. So I follow up by asking, "What was the most important new idea you gleaned from reading that book?" And now I have another deer in the headlights.

Still other leaders share in a straightforward and self-assured manner what they are reading and what they are getting out of it. That's a leader who is both a reader and a learner. And if you dig a little deeper inside this kind of leader you will almost always find a level of proactivity or "intentionality" to their reading. So let me ask you again—have you read any good books lately?

John R. Mott: A Historical Model

One of my favorite historical mentors is John Mott, the leader of the Student Volunteer Movement for over thirty years. Mott was a reader and a learner. On one 17-day voyage to South Africa, he booked a second cabin on the steamship just for his books! Mott sat on the deck of the ship reading one book after another. An opinionated leader, he was observed ripping pages out of books he didn't agree with and "flinging them into the sea." On at least one 10-day trip, John Mott read almost an entire book each morning before feeling up to writing letters and reports.

What Makes a Good Read?

Remember the last time you were disappointed by a book? What makes a good read, and how can I maximize my time and resources when it comes to learning through reading? I've been asking myself that question and sought to organize my thoughts. I believe the right combination of content, format, style, timing, and approach makes the best opportunity to read and learn.

- *Content.* I know it is not very profound, but if the author doesn't have much of value to say it will be hard to harvest a great deal from the book. You would think the publisher ought to be your ally in screening out poor content, but plenty of fluff gets printed and promoted these days. But what if you get going on a book that turns out to be disappointing from the perspective of content? I believe it is the author's responsibility to engage my mind and stir my heart. Don't allow yourself to get bogged down with a bad book. It's amazing how many people feel some sort of moral obligation to finish a book, no matter how disappointing it may be, before they move on to the next title. Learn to find the balance between giving up on a book too early and bogging down in a quagmire of disinterest or disappointment.

• *Format.* Books come in a variety of formats including biographical, inspirational, devotional, instructional, recreational, etc. (By format I'm obviously not referring to fiction/nonfiction or hardcover/paperback.) While it is ideal to develop an appreciation for a wide

> **It's amazing how many people feel some moral obligation to finish a book, no matter how disappointing it may be.**

variety of formats, most people gravitate toward one or two. And authors tend to stick with a specific format as well. I prefer biographical and instructional formats. I don't do much of any reading in the inspirational, devotional, or recreational formats. (By devotional I'm referring to a genre of writing, not the personal time spent in worship, prayer, and the study of Scripture.) When good content is combined with one of my favorite formats I know I'm building momentum for a good read.

• *Style.* Some authors use flowery word pictures and lots of illustrative material while others write in a more natural or conversational style. The format of the book often dictates to some extent the style the author will choose. I like illustrative material but not when it gets in the way of the content. I prefer a conversational style of writing where I can almost imagine the author speaking out loud to me as I read. I like charts and graphs in more technical books to give visual depictions of the concepts. I have found some very popular authors whose books have sold extremely well write mostly in an inspirational or devotional format with a style that is harder for me to digest. I don't tend to buy this type of book although I know many other leaders who purchase everything these authors write.

• *Timing.* In some cases the only thing between me and a good read is the timing of what is happening in my life when I pick it up. We have all had people enthusiastically recommend a book as "life-changing" only to be disappointed upon purchasing it. Six months later the same book can become life changing for me too. Why? It's all about timing.

• *Approach.* The people I know who benefit most consistently from reading books have an approach to reading that is intentional if not explicit and preconceived. Leaders who are both readers and learners have an approach to reading that enables them to get the most out of the material and develop systems that enable them to utilize what they learn well into the future.

One Approach to Reading Right

I have met very few younger leaders with a well-developed approach to reading books that maximizes the potential for learning. So let me share with you how I'm seeking to read and learn with the goal of inspiring you to develop a system that works for you.

Before You Read

Ask the following questions of a book before you get into reading it:

• Why do I want to read this and what do I hope to get out of it? (There is nothing wrong with reading a book for fun. That in itself is what you hope to get out of it. Knowing what your purpose is will almost always enhance the value that comes from reading a book.)

• What is the subject of this book, and how much do I already know about it? (Obviously if you are new to the subject matter you will need to process the information differently than if you have a lot of expertise in a given area.)

• For whom was this book written? Who is the target audience? (Knowing who tit was written for helps you understand how hard you are going to have to work to apply the principles to your situation. A book written about marketing to corporate heavy hitters will require some careful processing when applying the ideas to a very small nonprofit organization.)

• What is the format of the book and the style of the author's writing? (In most cases the title and flyleaf copy will answer this question, but you may need to adjust your opinion after you get into the book.)

- Based on the above information, at what level should I interact with this book? (If you know a lot about a subject, you may simply want to scan or browse through the book looking for new ideas or helpful illustrations. If it is a subject you really need to dig in to you may want to read it word-for-word or even study it by reviewing portions of it several times.)

Note: In some cases you may decide not to read a book at all after answering these basic questions. I like to approach reading a book like I would attend a seminar. I'd never go to a seminar without giving some thought to what I hope to get out of it, who it is for, and what I already know about the topic.

While You Are Reading

Devise a system that works for you to identify the key concepts from the book so that you can readily process and utilize them later. I typically look for ideas, research/facts, quotes, and illustrations. (If the book is biographical I look for process items—how God was shaping this person; pivot points—the key turning point moments in their journey; and heart-stirring vignettes—the biographical equivalent of an illustration.)

I mark these various items as I read and transfer the page number to one of the blank pages in the front of the book along with what it is— quote, illustrations, etc. This allows for a much easier review of what I want to harvest after I have finished the book.

After You Have Finished

If you have invested a few hours interacting with a book it is important to bring closure to the process in an intentional manner. Here are a few questions to consider when closing out a book.

- Do I need to engage this material at another level? (Sometimes a book you intended to browse through may turn out to be worth reading or even studying. Sometimes the author will quote another source that piques your interest and is worth pursuing.)
- What are the most important ideas I have gleaned from this book, and how can I apply them?

- What research, data, or facts have I gleaned from this book? How can it help me?

- What quotes have I gleaned that are worth keeping?

- What illustrations have I gleaned that are worth keeping?

- How would I rate this book against others dealing with the same subject? Would I recommend this book to others interested in this subject?

If you want to keep growing you will need to find a way to learn from what you read. My approach might not work for you without some modification. Find an approach that enables you to maximize the benefits that come from reading good books, and use it.

With that in mind... have you read any good books lately?

WORKING IT OUT

Ideas for Application and Reflection

1. Do you have a system for maximizing what you read? If not, what aspects of the system I use would work for you?

2. How many books have you read so far this year? Do you see a pattern in terms of format, style, and topic?

3. What system do you use to retain and retrieve information from the books you read? Is it working?

4. What was the last book you read? What did you get out of it?

STRATEGIC
FORMATION

Leadership: Status or Servanthood

"Status is one of the primary non-monetary rewards of leadership; sometimes it is the main reward."

—Tom Marshall

A lot has been made in recent years about the benefits of "flattening" the organizational structure and dismantling the old-style command and control framework for leadership. If you have done any reading in the area of organizational design or had a conversation with a consultant in the past few years, you no doubt understand this trend. The infusion of younger leaders into the church and business workforce has contributed to the flattening of organizational structures and the redrawing of boxes with concentric circles on the organizational chart.

But no matter how creative the newly designed organizational chart looks or how "X-er friendly" the policy manual may be, removing status from an organizational culture is not easy. Like a computer virus in a hard drive, status embeds itself into the operating system of an organization, and simply deleting a few files won't get the job done. Tom Marshall, in his book *Understanding Leadership,* says, "Status is one of the primary non-monetary rewards of leadership; sometimes it is the main reward." I believe he is right. And I've been thinking a lot about the subject of status lately, for a few personal reasons.

First, I was scheduled to attend a global consultation in Jerusalem over the Christmas and New Year's holiday. But the event was canceled one week before my planned departure. After scrambling to make the best of the situation with my tickets (my wife Sherry was coming with me) I discovered that *not* going to Jerusalem meant I probably wouldn't qualify for United Airlines Premier Executive frequent flyer status for that year. What? No more free upgrades? No more moving to the top of the wait list? No more early boarding, quickly by-passing the peons in the waiting area? No more Gold Card to pull out of my travel wallet at the check-in counter? Me—Steve Moore—a mere traveling mortal? The thought of it was more than I could bear.

Then I remembered the deal I just made with my travel agent to take a few free tickets from her in place of my normal Red Carpet membership —something she has given me for free the past two years. I have come to expect the more secluded and comfortable environment in which to pull out my Palm Pilot or my laptop and check email while running through O'Hare—not to mention the international lounges where I feast on tiny sandwiches and drink free coffee while waiting for my flight to be announced. I couldn't help but think, *This is going to be a tough year.*

All kidding aside, I have to confess that status—even the Premier Executive or Red Carpet kind—can be addictive. And as much as I like the perks associated with these programs, it is the status that comes with them that has a seductive lure. So in the wake of this personal trauma and the responsibilities I have with Top Flight Leadership to help shape our budding organizational culture, I have been thinking quite a bit about status and leadership.

Leadership Status Symbols

Tom Marshall says, "Status is about our ranking or position in society in comparison or in relation to others." Status is that unwritten yet very real "pecking order" that helps us know who is more important than who in a given organizational culture or relational network. I am working on a simplified list of status symbols. Keep in mind that this does not apply to every situation across the board. But where people use these "special" conditions to elevate themselves or create a distinction between themselves and others it may well become a status symbol.

- *Special Position*—usually denoted by way of a title or place on the organizational chart or inclusion in an insider/elitist network.

Recently the pastor of a large church I know of changed his title from Pastor to Bishop. And he is careful to ensure that people refer to him as Bishop So-and-So. I can't see his heart, but I can't help wondering if the change had anything to do with all the special guest speakers he had coming to his church under the title of Bishop. To be sure there are a lot of people getting help at that church. But I have to confess the title change smells a bit like a status symbol.

Another more subtle form of status is the purposeful name-dropping leaders do to ensure those around them realize "I'm on the inside." This happens on and off the platform. There is a big difference between building a network and using your real or not-so-real connections to impress others or elevate your perceived status.

- *Special Privileges*—usually denoted by favorable or unique treatment others do not receive.

Just this week I spoke with a friend who found himself in the middle of a mess when a leader close to him with status was caught in moral failure. The most difficult part of the whole ordeal was the fact that leaders in the system were prepared to give a proverbial "slap on the wrist" and look the other way simply because of the status of the person involved. One of the younger leaders close to the mess asked the key decision-maker what would happen to him if he were caught in the same situation? The obvious answer was he would be thrown out on his ear (when he really should be restored—but that is another issue altogether.) Status can be a powerful force, even in the face of blatant sin.

- *Special Perks*—usually denoted by the biggest office, the best desk, the best view, the private bathroom, the closest parking space....

In the corporate world you can walk into a major office complex and without even looking at the name plates on the door you can identify the president's office, and the pecking order of the VP's simply by looking at where they are located, how big the room is, and what kind of furniture is in the office. Okay, more than a few churches and ministries operate like this too.

- *Special Preference*—usually denoted by deference given to ideas—even when they are outside the leader's area of expertise.

What keeps followers silent when the leader is speaking nonsense about a subject he or she knows nothing about? The awe and power of status. Some leaders court and protect status just for this kind of trump card in a planning or brainstorming meeting. There is a difference between "the buck stops here" and "my ideas have more value than yours because I have status and you don't." Leaders must make hard decisions. Someone has to be in charge. But no one has to have special status in order to function as the leader.

The Effect of Status on Leaders and Followers

Some of you may be reading this and saying to yourself, "Isn't this the way it is supposed to be?" Not necessarily. But before we get to that, let's look for a moment at how status impacts people. When status based leadership is at work…

- *Leaders may become vulnerable to pride, ego, vanity, and conceit.* More than one leader has started to believe his or her own press clippings and lost sight of a servant model of leadership due to status.

- *Leaders may become vulnerable to an unhealthy sense of ownership and attachment to their position (and the status symbols it brings).* It can be very difficult to let go of your spiritual Premier Executive status. Just ask King Saul.

- *Followers may become unwilling to cross the status barrier to hold leaders accountable for their performance or character.* How else can you explain the willingness of people to ignore blatant sin in leaders around them—except for the power of status?

- *Followers may accept status symbols as normative and perpetuate a two-tiered system in future ministry structures.* If you are struggling with whether or not there is anything wrong with status-based leadership, you probably fit here.

> **The best way to find out whether you really have a servant's heart is to see what your reaction is when you are treated like one.**

Status or Servanthood?

So the real question here is whether or not status-based leadership is compatible with servant leadership? Not if you want Jesus as your leadership role model. No one more intentionally rejected status-based leadership than Jesus. Have you read John 13 lately? I agree wholeheartedly with Tom Marshall's bottom line on status:

Leadership is a special function, but it has no special status.

Elizabeth Elliot said, "The best way to find out whether you really have a servant's heart is to see what your reaction is when somebody treats you like one." Have you been treated like a servant lately? How did you respond? If you take leadership away from a servant leader, what do you have left? A servant.

WORKING IT OUT

Ideas for Application and Reflection

1. How do you feel about status-based leadership—not just the concept overall, but the specific issue of status symbols and servant leadership?

2. Reflect on my working list of leadership status symbols. What would you add to this list?

3. What leaders (both contemporary and historical)—besides Jesus—do you think best modeled status-free leadership?

4. Reflect on the organizational culture in which you now serve. Rate it on a scale of 1–10 based leadership status symbols (1 being no status and 10 being completely dominated by status). Be alert to the fact that well-intentioned, even godly leaders can be duped into status-based leadership. Be cautious of a critical or judgmental spirit.

18

Status-Busting Leadership

> "I urge you to imitate me. [Timothy] will remind you of my way of life in Christ Jesus which agrees with what I teach everywhere in every church."
>
> **—Paul**

I have heard more than one minister/speaker quote Paul's words from 1 Corinthians 4:16, "I urge you to imitate me." But rarely is this verse connected with the passages that surround it. Verses 8–13 outline what life was like for an apostle in Paul's day. It's quite a laundry list—on display, condemned to die, made a spectacle, made fools for Christ, left weak, dishonored, hungry, thirsty, in rags, treated brutally, left homeless, hardworking, cursed, slandered… yes, the scum of the earth, the refuse of the world. Sure, Paul, sign me up.

And on the heels of this list Paul says the unthinkable—"Imitate me." If that wasn't enough, he is going to send Timothy, who can testify to Paul's way of life.

Not exactly a status-conscious leader, this apostle Paul. Why do we applaud this kind of leadership "back then" and reject it "here-and-now"?

The Bible and Status

King David shunned status like few leaders ever have. Here are a few examples:

- After killing Goliath, David was entitled to marry King Saul's oldest daughter. This would have brought him great status as the son-in-law of the king. But he responded saying, "'Who am I, and what is my family or my father's clan in Israel, that I should become the king's son-in-law?'" (1 Samuel 18:18). When the time came, David passed, and Merab was given to someone else.

- Saul's other daughter, Michal, was in love with David and pressed her case with her father. Saul was devious in his motives but had his attendants tell David, "Look, the king is pleased with you, and attendants all like you; now become his son-in-law" (1 Samuel 18:22). But David replied to them saying, "'Do you think it is a small matter to become the king's son-in-law? I'm only a poor man and little known'" (verse 23). Obviously David had not been reading his own press clippings—"Saul has slain his thousands, and David his tens of thousands." He did eventually pay for his marriage with Michal with a hundred Philistine foreskins. But he was not easily enticed with instant status that would come from being the son-in-law of the king.

- One of the spoils of David's victory over Goliath was the sword he was carrying at the time of his death. David used this sword to behead Goliath, and he is the last one to have it when that part of the narrative closes. A status-conscious leader would have found a way to display this trophy of personal triumph for all to see. Can you hear it? "Yeah, that's the sword I took from Goliath after I killed him. I cut off his own head with it—to God be all the glory." (Even status-hungry leaders sneak that phrase in for effect.)

- But not David. In 1 Samuel 21 David is running for his life from Saul. He stops to visit the priest at Nob and gets bread for his men. David asked the priest, "'Don't you have a spear or sword here?'... 'The priest replied, 'The sword of Goliath the Philistine, whom you killed in the Valley of Elah, is here; it is wrapped in a cloth behind the ephod. If you want it, take it; there is no sword here but that one.'" The obvious question is how did this incredible symbol of personal triumph that rightfully belonged to David end up wrapped in a cloth behind the ephod? I believe it had something to do with the fact David was not hungry for status symbols.

- In 1 Chronicles 11 David found himself in battle once again with the Philistines. In a moment of exhaustion he cried out saying, "'Oh, that someone would get me a drink of water from the well near the gate of Bethlehem!'" One problem. David had some very loyal and brave followers who were willing to risk their lives to get their leader a drink. They carried a pitcher of water back to David. "But he refused to drink it; instead, he poured it out before the Lord. 'God forbid that I should do this!' he said. 'Should I drink the blood of these men who went at the risk of their lives?'" David was clearly embarrassed by the whole thing. His leadership was a special function but it carried no special status.

So in David we have a glimpse of what status-free leadership might look like. But how can we flesh this out in the here-and-now? Here are a few questions you may find helpful.

Dismantling Status in Your Organizational Culture

When evaluating position, privileges, perks, preference, power, priorities, promotion, prejudice, and anything else that smacks of status, ask the following questions.

- Do I need this [fill in the blank—bigger office, special parking space, private bathroom...] to do my job more effectively? Some CEOs have lots of meetings that require privacy, with individuals and various teams. It may well be the best way to deal with this special function is to have a little larger office with a small table. The bottom line is function—do I need this to be more effective?

- Is this [fill in the blank again] a legitimate reward for my performance? Status-free organizational cultures need not be experiments in socialism or sameness. There is nothing wrong with paying the top leader more or providing a system of motivation that is performance based. (Unless, of course, other members of the team are excluded from a properly prorated system.)

- Does this [fill in the blank] create a separation (real or perceived) between me and me those I am leading?

- Does this [fill in the blank] increase my vulnerability to pride and egocentrism?

- Would this [fill in the blank] make it hard for me to let go of my leadership role, even if I knew God was directing it? Would I be tempted to use fleshly means to hold on to my place of leadership in order to retain this special...?

Status-Busting Behaviors

If you are serious about creating a status-free organizational culture, try adding some of these to your present and future leadership behaviors. Keep in mind, almost everyone without status is against it. What will happen to you when you have it is the real question.

- *Don't use titles unless you have to.* Okay, every once in a while you will find yourself on the platform of a formal meeting in Asia or Africa where you will need to give in to the preferred introduction of the very Reverend, Doctor, Bishop, Your Excellency, blah, blah, blah. But most of the time you will be able to go by your first name. Use it.

- *Sit in the middle of the table instead of the head.* Why do leaders feel they have to sit at the head of the table whenever they have a meeting? Try sitting in the middle of one side or the other when you hold a meeting.

> " Everyone without status is against it. What will happen to you when you have it is the real question. "

- *Don't flaunt your trophies.* Put the sword you used to kill Goliath in cloth behind the ephod. Or if it needs to be on display put it in a common area and make it a team trophy with group ownership.

- *Answer the phone.* If you want to discern the pecking order of three leaders from an organization just look at who is expected to answer the phone in that time when the secretaries are all in the bathroom. Surprise everyone and answer the phone. It will make a statement.

- *Show up for the grunt work.* "The big board meeting is coming and we need to do a major cleanup around here. But unfortunately I have to attend such and such a meeting on those days. I'm counting on you guys to do a good job." Sound familiar? Leaders need to steward their gifts properly and use their time wisely. It will not be possible or appropriate to work alongside the janitor every day just to prove you are status-free. But when the big deal goes down and others who would not normally be swinging a hammer or pushing a broom are doing so at your request—join them.

- *Become vulnerable and accountable to your team.* Put status on the table and allow everyone to ask you questions when it appears you are losing focus on true servant leadership. Be sure to explain the function behind special circumstances when they come up.

WORKING IT OUT

Ideas for Application and Reflection

1. Evaluate your organization for status-based leadership using the questions articulated in this article. How do your conclusions compare to what you came up with on the 1–10 scale included with the previous article?

2. What other Bible characters or passages could you cite that demonstrate a status-free leadership style? Share some of these ideas/passages with your team and ask for feedback.

3. Which of the above status-busting behaviors would be the hardest for you? Share your answer with a ministry colleague or accountability partner and ask for their help in breaking free.

4. What is the most important step you could take to move toward a status-free organizational culture?

19

Emotional Intelligence

"Without [emotional intelligence] a person can have the best training in the world, an incisive analytical mind... but he still won't make a great leader."

—Daniel Goleman

What is the "must have" characteristic of highly effective leaders? That is a question that would stir quite a bit of debate in most leadership circles. One idea that I would not expect to hear is that of emotional intelligence.

At lower levels of leadership the issues of ability, intelligence, training, and experience play a major role in distinguishing good leaders from very good leaders. But the higher you move up the leadership ladder, the less these threshold components—ability, intelligence, training, experience—matter in terms of separating the good from the great.

Think of professional athletes for example. When they played at the high school level, many pro athletes were head and shoulders above everyone else in their league, let alone their team. But when they got to college, the difference between them and other players was somewhat diminished. By the time they get to the pros, the difference is even less noticeable.

The same is true for leaders. At the highest levels of leadership, the distinguishing factor, which separates good leaders from great leaders, is not primarily their training or I.Q. but—according to Daniel Goleman—their emotional intelligence. In fact, Goleman asserts that, "Without it a person can have the best training in the world, an incisive analytical mind and an endless supply of smart ideas but he still won't make a great leader."

Evaluating Emotional Intelligence

Goleman studied research on the competency models of 188 different companies ranging from Lucent Technologies to British Airways. The research evaluated the competency of leaders based on cognitive skills (analytical thinking, big picture perspective), technical skills (accounting, systems), and emotional intelligence (working with others, managing change). It was through this study that he concluded emotional intelligence is twice as important as other factors, and its relevance increased proportionately with movement up the leadership ladder. Those in the study with higher levels of emotional intelligence out-produced others both inside and outside the United States. (In other words, they believe this research is not culture-bound.)

Five Components of Emotional Intelligence

Goleman suggests there are five basic components of Emotional Intelligence:

- *Self-Awareness*—Leaders with emotional intelligence know who they are, where they are going, and why. They have a deep understanding of their emotions, strengths, weaknesses, needs, and drives. They are honest with themselves. They make decisions that are consistent with their values. They set goals—short-term and long—that flow from who they are and where they want to go. They operate with candor and are willing to admit failure. They receive constructive criticism and willingly ask for help.

Implications for Christian leaders: Leaders with emotional intelligence are making progress in destiny processing. They are refining an explicit philosophy of leadership (ministry), which empowers their decision-making. They have a learning posture, which fuels a teachable spirit.

Want to be a great leader? How are you doing in the area of destiny processing? Refining your ministry philosophy? Personal growth?

- *Self-Regulation*—Leaders with emotional intelligence are in control of their feelings and impulses. They have mastered their emotions to the extent that they are able to deal with the unpredictable or even disastrous circumstances of life on an even keel. They radiate an environment of trust, safety, and loyalty. Their followers are not afraid to be the one to bring bad news. They are thoughtful and reflective enough to navigate the moguls of life in proper balance.

Implications for Christian leaders: Leaders who want to be effective at the highest levels of Christian leadership are passionate about allowing the fruits of the Holy Spirit—including patience and self-control—to be seen in their daily activities.

Want to be a great leader? How would your followers (including your family) rate you when it comes to self-control? How about patience?

- *Motivation*—Leaders with emotional intelligence have an inner drive to go beyond the minimum expectations of others. They have a desire to improve, to do things better. They want to keep score so as to be able to measure growth or improvement. They have a buy-in to the organization, which expresses itself in loyalty to the cause.

Implications for Christian leaders: Christian leaders need a passion that expresses itself in a sense of responsibility. Passion can cover a multitude of sins when it comes to the lack of ability or training. I have seen very average communicators take the house down based purely on the fact they were passionate about what they said and communicated a sense of personal responsibility for the cause.

Want to be a great leader? When was the last time you cried over the cause? Is your passion meter stuck on "whatever"?

- *Empathy*—Leaders with emotional intelligence thoughtfully consider the feelings of followers in the process of making decisions. They are not governed by this empathy so as to keep them from making the tough call. But they recognize they are dealing with people and that actions have consequences. They go beyond trite statements like "Deal with it" or "Get over it" when helping followers process

> **Effective Christian leaders realize the most preferred power base is spiritual authority.**

change. This kind of empathy is critical in an environment where teams bring with them complex relationships and globalization requires cross-cultural communication. Effective mentoring and coaching on the job grows out of the strength of relationship, which is enhanced by empathetic interaction.

Implications for Christian leaders: What Goleman describes as empathy could easily be viewed as servant leadership. Effective Christian leaders realize the most preferred power base is spiritual authority, which flows from strength of character and servant attitudes.

Want to be a great leader? Try living the Golden Rule. What is your default power base setting?

- *Social Skills*—Leaders with emotional intelligence are purposefully friendly. They are not necessarily sanguine in their personality type. But they are intentional about cultivating interpersonal communication skills. They have an "others" focus that makes it easy to carry on a conversation. They readily seek common ground and ask sincere questions.

Implications for Christian Leaders: The social skills Goleman describes have a common root in listening. Being a good listener is not always at the top of the priority list of high-energy leaders. Many times as leaders we are busy forming our rebuttal statement after the first three words have been spoken to us.

Social skills in this context are really a combination of other aspects of emotional intelligence. These skills emerge as the components of emotional intelligence are put to work synergistically in real life.

Want to be a great leader? Cultivate good listening habits. Be quick to listen and slow to speak.

Final Comments

Let me take you back to the opening thoughts in this article. What is the "must have" characteristic of highly effective leaders? If you were in a room with other leaders and that question was asked, I predict few, if any, would have answered emotional intelligence.[1] And as a result, few of the practical application comments flowing from this article would have been on our short list of action steps. Review them for a minute... should they be?

- Want to be a great leader? How are you doing in the area of destiny processing? Refining your ministry philosophy? Personal growth?

---

[1] Goleman has updated his research and now has only four categories, listed in more recent publications as Self-Awareness, Self-Management, Social Awareness, and Relationship Management.

• Want to be a great leader? How would your followers (including your family) rate you when it comes to self-control? How about patience?

• Want to be a great leader? When was the last time you cried over the cause? Is your passion meter stuck on "whatever"?

• Want to be a great leader? Try living the Golden Rule. What is your default power base setting?

• Want to be a great leader? Cultivate good listening habits. Be quick to listen and slow to speak.

WORKING IT OUT

Ideas for Application and Reflection

1. Do you agree with Daniel Goleman's assertion that emotional intelligence is the most important distinguishing factor between high-level leaders?

2. Can you think of a high-level leader who is/was very successful but did not have emotional intelligence? If yes, who? Did they succeed because of this lack of emotional intelligence or in spite of it?

3. What component of emotional intelligence is least valued by traditional leadership paradigms?

4. Rate yourself on a scale of 1–20 in each component of emotional intelligence. Then total your score for each area—a perfect score would total 100.

5. Based on your answer to number 4, which component of emotional intelligence do you most need to develop?

20

Living Life on Purpose

"The highest expression of destiny awareness is a personal mission statement."

There is a story of a German philosopher who took a stroll one evening to ponder the meaning of life. With disheveled hair and dressed in ragged clothes he wandered in the rain through dimly lit streets in a state of deep reflection. The police came upon him, and, because he looked suspicious, they abruptly cornered him asking, "Who are you?" and "Where are you going?" To which the philosopher replied, "Those are the very questions I'm trying to answer. Can you help me?"

Of course the police and the philosopher were looking at these questions on two completely different levels. And frankly these two questions that get to the heart of destiny processing—who are you? where are you going?—will be answered in radically different ways depending on your perspective.

Two Questions—Three Answers

There are really three different perspectives or vantage points from which these two questions—who am I? where I am going?—can be viewed.

- *Temporal Perspective*—The temporal perspective focuses on the here and now of life. If you ask someone "Who are you?" and "Where are you going?" from the temporal perspective you are expecting a name and a location. The fact is you can't get by in life without paying attention to the temporal perspective. Just ask the German philosopher.

- *Eternal Perspective*—The eternal perspective is focused on the reality of an afterlife that extends beyond time and space. If you asked a Christian leader these two questions from the eternal perspective you would hope to hear, "I'm a child of God and I'm going to the place my Lord Jesus said he would prepare for me." There are many seasons of life and leadership where having an eternal perspective enables us to deal with the challenges of the here and now.

- *Missional Perspective*—The missional perspective focuses on everything in between the temporal and eternal. It addresses the fact that we were destined by God for a life of meaningful service here on the earth before we go to be with Him forever. Bruce Wilkinson addressed the missional perspective with these words, "If the God of heaven loves you infinitely and wants you in His presence every moment, and if He knows that heaven is a much better place for you, then why on earth has He left you here?" He left you here so you could cooperate with Him to build the Kingdom. That is the missional perspective.

Destiny Defined

I have defined *destiny* as the sovereign purpose for which you have been created that, when fulfilled, brings God the greatest glory, brings you the greatest joy, and most significantly advances the Kingdom. This is the ultimate win/win situation. As your destiny is fulfilled God receives maximum glory, you receive maximum joy, and the Kingdom is most strategically advanced. There is nothing you could do that would bring God more glory than to fulfill the purposes for which you were created. Jesus alluded to this in John 17:4 saying, "I have brought you glory on the earth by completing the work you gave me to do."

> **There is nothing you could do that would bring God more glory than to fulfill the purposes for which you were created.**

In pursuing destiny fulfillment we receive maximum joy because there is nothing in all the world that can compete with the adventure God has mapped out for you. In your wildest, most imaginative and creative moment you could never think up something to do with your life that could compare with the destiny God has already designed. Joy is quite different than happiness or comfort. Destiny fulfillment may involve great hardship, suffering or even martyrdom. But in the midst of the pain that comes with obedience God gives unexplainable joy.

Destiny fulfillment is strategic in that it focuses our lives on the specific "good works" God has "prepared in advance for us to do" (Ephesians 2:10). If you really want to build the Kingdom, focus on destiny fulfillment.

The Destiny Formula

A subject as complex as destiny cannot be reduced to a formula with mathematic precision. But when looking at how the pieces of destiny come together, a formulaic framework can be helpful. Here's my version of a destiny formula:

history + identity + ministry = destiny

In the destiny formula, history deals with where I have come from, identity deals with who God made me to be, and ministry deals with what God has for me to do. Each variable in the destiny formula works together in a complementary fashion to enable us to see more clearly the destiny God has for us.

Destiny and Life Planning

Destiny awareness is the fuel that drives life planning. I've met lots of leaders who have gone through some form of life planning and perhaps even developed a personal mission statement. But when I ask them what their mission statement is I'm often met by a rather awkward pause and then a quick disclaimer—"It's been quite a while since I went to that workshop. I don't remember what I wrote offhand. But I know right where it is in my file cabinet." Is that what a mission statement is meant to do—fill up space in your filing system? I don't think so.

I believe life planning without a strong destiny awareness component can become mechanical and create a functional-disconnect between the mission statement and daily life. But you show me a leader who has a growing sense of destiny awareness—believing God has a unique purpose for his or her life—and I'll show you someone who is internally motivated to find out what that destiny is and how to fulfill it. The highest expression of destiny awareness is a personal mission statement.

Lowering the Bucket

Proverbs 20:5 says, "The purposes of a man's heart are deep waters, but a man of understanding draws them out." The phrase "draws them out" is a form of speech known as an idiom. The literal Hebrew refers to a bucket that is dangled or lowered into a well to draw out water. So the original language uses a play on words, referring to deep waters (purposes of the heart) and a bucket lowered to "draw them out."

This same Hebrew word for *purposes* is translated in other verses as plans, advice, counsel, strategy, and prediction. A loose paraphrase of Proverbs 20:5 emphasizing the meaning of this Hebrew word could be, "The guidance needed to make decisions and plan for the future God has ordained within a man's heart are deep waters, but a man of understanding draws them out."

God has put His purposes in your heart. And they are like deep waters. You will need to be a man or woman of understanding to draw them out. Processing the history, identity, and ministry variable of the destiny formula is like lowering the bucket to draw out the purposes of God for your life.

You need to "lower the bucket" and draw out these deep waters with the focus of developing a personal mission for at least three important reasons.

- *If you know your mission you can modify it on purpose.* A personal mission statement, especially for young leaders, is a dynamic statement that changes over time as more of God's plan is made clear. But how can you be intentional about modifying something you have never articulated?

- *If you know your personal mission you can use it as a filter in making decisions.* When you are sorting through your options for training and ministry it is empowering to be able to process those opportunities in light of what you know about who you are and where you are going as expressed in a personal mission statement.

- *If you know your personal mission you can model living life on purpose for other leaders.* Your growing sense of focus and passion for who you are and where you are going will have a powerful impact on those who follow you. You will be more effective in leading them towards

God's purposes for the group, and your followers will develop a hunger to discover who God made them to be. But how can you help others with the missional perspective when you haven't sorted it out yourself?

WORKING IT OUT

Ideas for Application and Reflection

1. Review the journey of the following Bible characters: Jacob, Joseph, John the Baptist, and Paul. To what extent were they aware of their destiny? How did God make it known to them?

2. Destiny awareness can have a downside. How was this fact reflected in Moses' life? (Hint—Read Acts 7:25.)

3. How could destiny awareness, in the form of a personal mission statement, serve as a filter for major life decisions?

4. Which of the variables in the destiny formula do you need to spend time processing? Who do you know that could help coach you in this strategic area?

21
Marriage and Destiny:
Part 1

"I came to feel that part of my mission in life, one of the objects of my being, was to make some one little woman happy."

—Samuel Logan Brengle

It is generally not that difficult to get leaders—even younger leaders—to pay attention when speaking about issues such as destiny and life mission. Leaders intuitively understand that being successful (regardless of how you define it) is at least in part a function of knowing where you are going and how you plan to get there. Even leaders who don't have a mission statement or understanding of destiny tend to realize they need to grow in this area or risk falling short of their potential.

Yet it is this same focus on mission, destiny, and life objectives that can pull leaders (more often men) from their spouses and drive a wedge in the most important foundation of effective leadership—the social base. *Social base* is the *Leadership Emergence Theory* term that describes a leader's relational foundation, including the home in which he or she grew up as well as the home being built through marriage. That is why I find these words of Samuel Logan Brengle so refreshing: "I came to feel that part of my mission in life, one of the objects of my being, was to make some one little woman happy." Having embraced marriage, he saw a part of his life mission (one of the objects of my being) as being integrally connected with making his wife happy. (By happy he really meant fulfilled or complete. Happiness for Samuel Logan Brengle was inseparable with holiness. After all, he was a Salvation Army leader!)

Brengle has been an inspiring historical mentor for me in many different ways. He was a great leader with a lot of spiritual authority. He was a powerful communicator with an international itinerant platform. His life example continues to shape my understanding of public ministry. He was a Bible-centered leader whose ministry was founded on the power of God's Word.

Brengle was once asked the following question by a field officer, "If you had but ten minutes to prepare for a meeting, how would you spend it?" Brengle responded with two words, "In prayer!" He could answer like this because his spirit was thoroughly saturated with the Bible. He had spent years pouring over the pages of God's Word. He was asked by a young theologian, "What preparation do you make for preaching?" He responded saying, "My lifetime has been a preparation for preaching... to warm others—and is that not your purpose in preaching?—a man must keep the fire burning hot in his own soul."

So you can see Brengle was a fiery leader with lots of passion for the ministry God gave him. Yet he was also committed to fulfilling that part of his mission that came with being a husband. No matter how noble or Kingdom-worthy your mission might be, if you are married you must figure out how to merge that destiny with your spouse.

It Begins With Love

The driving motivation to fully integrate your destiny with your spouse is the willful choice (as opposed to the emotion) you have made to love your spouse unconditionally until separated by death. If you don't keep the flames of your commitment to love your spouse alive, the motivation to partner together in ministry will not likely be high on the mission priority list.

Brengle is a wonderful example of this loving commitment. Here is how he described his "latest autobiography" to his wife Lily:

> See here, Mrs. Lily Swift Samuel Logan Brengle, I love you till I hardly know what to do with myself! I'm awfully in love, hopelessly in love, head over heels in love, and altogether in love. No help for me! I never expect to get over it. I'm swallowed alive and whole in love—engulfed deep, no way of escape—overpowered, enveloped, and buried in love. There's my latest autobiography. That's the heart of it!

Do you love your spouse like this? If you have made the decision to marry, keeping this fire of love alive in your heart is an essential component of effective ministry over the long haul and a vital part of fulfilling your life mission.

The greatest safety net you will ever have to protect you from moral failure is a "white-hot" passion for your spouse flowing from a willful choice you have made to love him or her unconditionally unto death.

Merging Destiny With Your Spouse

I've thought a lot about this subject, and my wife Sherry and I are still working through this process ourselves. Here are some basic principles we are finding helpful that I've shared with other couples.

Seek to discover your destiny as an individual before merging with your spouse. I advise couples to pursue destiny processing, culminating in a personal mission statement, before trying to blend a sense of mission as a couple. Your oneness as a couple does not undo your uniqueness as an individual.

Bring your destiny together with your spouse's in the following stages:

- *Stage 1:* What do we have in *common*? While it is true that opposites often attract when it comes to marriage, there is almost always something you will find your destiny has in common with your spouse. Be sure to get beyond the formal mission statement to the causes/activities about which you are passionate. There is always overlap in the area of children and most often in the area of church.

- *Stage 2:* How is my mission *complementary* to that of my spouse? Even if your mission seems quite different from your spouse, or if you find very little common ground, you may discover ways destiny fulfillment for you will complement the mission of your spouse.

- *Stage 3:* How can we *compromise* in order for both of us to fulfill our mission? Two major areas of compromise are timing and resources. You may discover it is impractical or even impossible for both of you to pursue graduate studies at the same time due to the lack of resources or responsibility for children. One spouse may face a decision to relocate as part of destiny fulfillment. You may find it helpful to put basic timelines together and revisit them often to keep the destiny dream alive in the heart of the spouse who has chosen to delay action for a later date.

- *Stage 4:* How will we deal with areas that appear to *conflict* with regard to destiny fulfillment? I specifically place this question as stage 4 because I believe properly engaging the other three stages will reduce this list from what it might appear to be at the outset. But I'm not so naïve as to suggest there will never be apparent conflicts when it comes to merging destiny with your spouse. So how do we reconcile these issues?

First of all, remember that no part of your destiny will ever trump your marriage promise. You will never be justified in walking away from your marriage based on the fact you need to in order to fulfill your God-appointed destiny. The responsibility of marriage trumps your ministry/destiny. Period.

Prayerfully ask God, "How can I be true to my marriage responsibility and still focus on my life mission and destiny?" Communicate to your spouse that your highest priority in ministry is marriage and you are committed to find a way to fulfill your marriage promise and your destiny. Be patient enough to give God time to work.

> **You will never be justified in walking away from your marriage to fulfill your God-appointed destiny.**

Sometimes areas of conflict are actually rooted in an imbalance connected with one of these three factors:

- *Selectivity Factor*—Some areas of conflict arise when one spouse has a very focused, narrow, or selective picture of destiny fulfillment. Is it possible a bigger picture or broader perspective of your mission may reduce the tension or erase the conflict?

- *Serenity Factor*—The lack of peace a spouse may be feeling due to other issues (such as distance from family, unsaved parent, wayward child, financial pressures, family illness, etc.) may actually be clouding the ability to process a viable compromise. Is it possible there is another issue that needs to be resolved in order for you both to have perspective on this apparent conflict?

- *Spirituality Factor*—In spite of our best intentions, married couples don't always experience growth at the same pace. Destiny or mission conflicts can arise when one spouse moves into a level of spiritual depth or maturity outside the range of the other. Is it possible the conflict is being exacerbated by an imbalance in the spiritual walk?

If you are married, one aspect of your mission is to make your spouse happy. Have you embraced that part of your life mission? Are you committed to merge your destiny with your spouse?

WORKING IT OUT

Ideas for Application and Reflection

1. If you are married, have your spouse read over this article. Then block out some time to discuss where you are in the process of merging your destiny with your spouse.

2. Consider doing a historical mentoring project with your spouse on this subject. I highly recommend the book *Hudson and Maria Taylor* as another inspiring love story that infuses a ministry partnership. The Brengle book is *Samuel Logan Brengle: Portrait of a Prophet,* written by Clarence Hall and published by the Salvation Army.

3. Give your spouse a Day Alone With God to process destiny issues. (Top Flight Leadership has a helpful resource on this issue called "Charting the Course." It is available from our website at www.TopFlight.org.)

4. Ask a seasoned ministry couple to mentor you in this area. Pick a date when you can get together and hear their story as well as share the issues you are facing now.

Marriage and Destiny: Part 2

"Will I ever find a man to love me like that?"

The Bible is full of classic love stories. One of my favorites is depicted in these words from Genesis 29:20, "Jacob served seven years to get Rachel, but they seemed like only a few days to him because of his love for her." Seven years is a long time. No matter how much you love someone. (And this story takes an even more bizarre twist when Jacob is tricked into marrying Rachel's sister first, only discovering the price for Rachel is another seven years of work!)

I've seen too many Christian leaders start off with a Jacob-like love for their spouse only to allow that fire to grow dim over time. The pressure of being in the spotlight as a Christian leader combined with increased attacks from the enemy make for a deadly combination. When the heat of the battle intensifies ministry leaders can find themselves trapped between what appears to be an either/or situation: Pursue the calling and risk the marriage, or pursue the marriage and risk the calling.

I believe ministry leaders need to balance the sense of zeal and passion they have for destiny fulfillment with two other important factors: reality and responsibility. By reality I am referring to the practical facts of the situation or circumstances of life. By responsibility I mean the obligations that come with commitments that have been made or naturally flow from the roles they have embraced as husband and perhaps father. Few leaders have modeled a God-honoring way to hold these issues in healthy tension more than Robertson McQuilkin. But before we get to his story, I'd like to share a bit of my own journey.

A Personal Testimony

After I sold out to Christ in my early twenties, God put me on a fast of sorts when it comes to relationships with the opposite sex. I had lived a life of unbelievable debauchery and needed a season of focus that kept my attention only on God. For more than two years I knew God was actively blocking me from entering any kind of relationship. I had only one date in that time, and it was clear God was saying no to my honest plea for a Christian girl.

By the time I got to Bible college I had come to the conclusion that God had called me to a life of celibacy. So it was a real problem when I first met Sherry—who is now my wife. I tried to deny how much I wanted to date her. I came to God and asked Him to either take away the feelings I had or clarify the celibacy issue once and for all. God spoke very clearly and said, "You have always felt it would be harder to live a life of celibacy than a life of purity in marriage. You are wrong. For you it would be harder to faithfully promise yourself—unconditionally and forever—to one woman than to remain single." I found that rather amusing at first

> **Zeal and passion should be balanced by two other important factors: reality and responsibility.**

and confusing the more I thought about it. I asked God for clarification. I will never forget the response.

God spoke to me and said marriage is forever. What are you going to do if the day after you wedding your wife is in an accident and comes away paralyzed for life? Will you rearrange your life priorities to feed her, change her diapers, bathe her, and love her until death do you part? That was a major reality check. My mind began to race with all the morbid possible disasters that could over take the emotional yearnings I had for Sherry at the time. And soon I came to the place of prayer saying, "God, maybe it would be better for me to remain single." To this He replied, "If you can come to terms with what it means to say 'till death do us part' you have my blessing to pursue marriage."

We have been married since 1984 and I have signed every meaningful note I've ever written to my wife with the simple phrase, "till death do us part." It is my way of restating that if the reality of my situation should ever change my responsibilities as a husband and father will not go away.

A Practical Example

While I have only had to ponder these deep issues from a hypothetical vantage point (praise God), others are living in them and providing a contemporary model of faithfulness in the storm. One of the most vivid and moving examples is that of Robertson and Muriel McQuilkin.

Dr. McQuilkin served for twenty-two years at Columbia Bible College and Seminary. His leadership as the president was effective and well respected around the globe. But when Muriel began to show signs of Alzheimer's at age 55, life began to change for the McQuilkins. Muriel's condition worsened. She became incapable of enduring even short periods of time away from her husband. Her behavior regressed to that of a young child.

Once while traveling together Dr. McQuikin found himself trying to appease Muriel during a two-hour layover in Atlanta. After responding to the same list of questions for the umpteenth time and jogging to keep up with Muriel on speed-walks through the terminal, Dr. McQuilkin found himself seated across from a well-dressed businesswoman working on her laptop. She mumbled something that appeared to be addressed to Roberson McQuilken but not loud enough to be understood. He politely responded saying, "Pardon?" She answered, "Oh, I was just asking myself, 'Will I ever find a man to love me like that?'"

During this journey with Alzheimer's Dr. McQuilkin struggled with the question of whether ministry or Muriel should be sacrificed. "Should I put the kingdom of God first and, for the sake of Christ and the Kingdom, arrange for institutionalization?" There were many voices—trusted and lifelong friends—who urged him to take this route saying, "Muriel would become accustomed to the new environment quickly."

Listen to his thoughts on this: "People who do not know me well have said, 'Well, you always said, "God first, family second, ministry third."' But I never said that. To put God first means that all the responsibilities he gives are first too."

The realities of his situation and responsibilities as a husband were in fact the very Kingdom priorities God wanted him to embrace. And he did. Here is a portion of the letter that was sent to Columbia's constituency announcing the transition.

> Twenty-two years is a long time. But then again, it can be shorter than one anticipates. And how do you say good-bye to friends you do not wish to leave?

The decision to come to Columbia was the most difficult I have had to make; the decision to leave twenty-two years later, though painful, was one of the easiest. It was almost as if God engineered the circumstances so that I had no alternatives. Let me explain.

My dear wife Muriel, has been in failing mental health for about 12 years. So far I have been able to carry both her ever-growing needs and my leadership responsibilities at Columbia. But recently it has become apparent that Muriel is contented most of the time she is with me and almost none of the time I am away from her. It is not just "discontent." She is filled with fear—even terror—that she has lost me and always goes in search of me when I leave home. So it is clear to me that she needs me now, full-time.

Perhaps it would help you understand if I shared with you what I shared in chapel at the time of the announcement of my resignation. The decision was made, in a way, 42 years ago when I promised to care for Muriel, "in sickness and in health… till death do us part." So, as I told the students and faculty, as a man of my word, integrity has something to do with it. But so does fairness. She has cared for me fully and sacrificially all these years; if I cared for her for the next forty years I would not be out of her debt. Duty, however, can be grim and stoic. But there is more: I love Muriel. She is a delight to me—her childlike dependence and confidence in me, her warm love, occasional flashes of that wit I used to relish so, her happy spirit and tough resilience in the face of her continual distressing frustration. I don't *have* to care for her. I *get* to! It is a high honor to care for so wonderful a person.

This amazing story is told in Dr. McQuilkin's book *A Promise Kept.* Here is an excerpt from the closing words:

Twenty summers ago, Muriel and I began our journey into the twilight. It's midnight now, at least for her. Sometimes I wonder when dawn will break… Yet, in her silent world Muriel is so content, so lovable… If Jesus took her home, how I would miss her gentle, sweet presence… I love to care for her. She's my precious.

Will your spouse ever have someone love them like that?

WORKING IT OUT

Ideas for Application and Reflection

1. Encourage your spouse to read this article. Together, rethink your value priority list when it comes to God, family, and ministry. How would you describe it to a young leader preparing for ministry?

2. Consider purchasing the book *A Promise Kept* (Tyndale) and read it—if you are married, with your spouse.

3. Develop a devotional or message on the priority of marriage that challenges young leaders with these issues.

4. Spend some time praying for a ministry leader you know who is facing a difficult time balancing the reality of his or her situation and the responsibilities that flow from being a spouse/parent.

23

Personal Change Management:
Guidance Processing

"You never completely solve your problems through change. You merely exchange your existing problems for a set of new ones you have come to prefer."

Life is filled with decisions about change. In one 60-day period last year I changed my ISP, changed my cell phone service, changed the oil in my van (well, actually, I paid someone else to do that), and... you get the picture. Most change management decisions flow quite naturally from our internal decision-making grid without a whole lot of inner turmoil. In spite of the fact the motivation for change usually arises from a desire to solve a problem or make something better, you never completely solve your problems through change. You merely exchange your existing problems for a set of new ones you have come to prefer.

But what I want to get at in this article is the kind of change that falls in the category of what I describe as a "life choice." Life choices are major decisions that impact how we fulfill our life mission and move toward destiny fulfillment. We're not talking here about the decision between restaurants—Outback's or Chevy's—but rather Oklahoma City or Chicago (yes, geographic change can have a powerful impact on life mission). What grid do we use to manage this kind of change? Somehow we have to find a balance between the mystical and the analytical, between prayer and planning. But how?

I believe having a sense of personal destiny marked by a clear and concise personal mission statement removes most of the fog when making life choices. But even when you have the airport in view you have to choose the runway on which you are supposed to land. Even when all the options before you match up with your life mission, you still need to be able to pull the trigger on one of them.

A few years ago I came across a guidance-processing matrix that I have shared with hundreds of young leaders struggling to make life choices. Over the last few months I've had a chance to use it again myself.

Guidance Processing Matrix

Hearing the Voice of God in the Heart	Hearing the Voice of God in the Church	Hearing the Voice of God in the Circumstances
(Inner Peace)	(Godly Counsel)	(Open and Closed Doors)
Hearing the Voice of God in the Word		

Note: I first encountered this matrix from Dr. J. Robert Clinton, who credits it to Frank Sells.

The entire matrix swings on the ability to hear God's voice. Few things are more critical to effective Christian leadership than hearing God. This is the cornerstone of vision and destiny. When leaders ask followers to begin a change process, one of the fundamental questions they will ask (albeit for some subconsciously) is, "Does my leader have a good track record of hearing from God?"

The more radical the change, or the more sacrifice required by followers, the more important it will be that they believe the leader really has heard from God. Few biblical leaders modeled this more than David. (First Samuel 23:1–6 is just one of many examples.) So how do leaders (or any believers) hear the voice of God? Let me take you through the guidance-processing matrix with some specific and personal illustrations from my personal journey.

- *Hearing God's voice in the Word.* This is the foundation of the matrix. Ultimately God leads us through His Word—which most often comes through the written text of the Bible. But I believe God still communicates through dreams, visions, and other revelatory means. Of course none of these should be viewed as equal to the Bible nor will they ever contradict what has been written in Scripture.

Personal illustration: On May 18, 2000, we had a day of prayer and fasting at Emerging Young Leaders, the mission with whom I was serving at the time. One of our staff members shared an article that had several references to 2 Kings. I opened my Bible and turned to one of those references from 2 Kings 8. My eyes fell on these words of Elisha, "'Go away with your family wherever you can'" (verse 1). In that moment I knew that God was speaking to me. Sherry and I had been dealing with a tremendous amount of pressure on our marriage and family due to the intensity of my ministry responsibilities. In just a few weeks I was scheduled to leave for a training experience in Europe. I knew God was trying to tell me my family life was out of balance and that some fairly radical steps would be needed to bring things back into proper alignment.

As I continued reading in that text I realized that Elisha was speaking to the Shunammite woman and that her withdrawal from Israel lasted seven years! I thought—"Oh Lord, if I take some radical step to focus on my family over my ministry for a long time I won't be able to re-enter at the same level of leadership and influence You have given me now. Would it be right to simply go off the map like that and squander the place of influence you have given me?" I guess you don't need me to explain how prideful and selfish that line of thinking was. But here is the amazing part.

God led me in the next few moments to the rest of this pas-

> **God was telling me my life was out of balance and radical steps would be needed to bring it back into alignment.**

sage. The Shunammite woman came back after seven years to beg the king to return her house and land. At that moment, Gehazi was talking to the king explaining the great things Elisha had done. Just when he told the king about Elisha raising the Shunammite woman's son from the dead she arrived. Gehazi told the king—"'This is the woman... this is her son who Elisha restored to life.'" The king asked her about it and she told him. Here is the real kicker—the king assigned an official to this woman's case saying, "'Give back everything that belonged to her, including all the income from her land from the day she left the country until now'" (2 Kings 8:5–6).

In that moment, I knew God was speaking to me again saying, "Steve, I could completely remove you from any public ministry for as long as I want and then bring you back into the picture not just where you were when you left but where you would have been if you had never left the scene at all." God, why are you so merciful to me? I know what it is to hear God's voice in the Word. I have May 18, 2000 written in the margin of my Bible and I won't forget what happened that day. Do you know what it is to hear God's voice?

- *Hearing God's voice in the heart* (This is what we often call inner peace.) In addition to His Word, God speaks to us in our hearts through the gentle, often indescribable, peace that enables us to know that we know God is leading and everything is okay. On the other hand, we have all had times when deep down in our spiritual gut we simply knew something wasn't right. And if you grew up around the church you probably learned to describe this by saying, "I just don't have peace about that." The lack of real peace is reason for caution.

Personal illustration: My summer in Europe was absolutely awesome—with one exception. For a good part of the trip every time I called home my wife cried on the phone. Sometimes we prayed together; sometimes I just listened to her vent. Thankfully by the end of the trip God was bringing a measure of perspective to both of us and our reunion was like honeymooners. But we both knew something needed to change.

- *Hearing God's voice in the church* (This is what we often call godly counsel.) I have been blessed beyond measure with wise mentors (both upward and peer) who have given strategic counsel at just the right time.

Personal illustration: After our whirlwind summer we began to meet with another couple here in town for prayer and counsel. We had six sessions with a professional counselor recommended by our pastor and we involved some key intercessors around the country. They sharpened and validated many of the lessons we felt God was teaching us and affirmed the action steps we began to take as a couple.

- *Hearing God's voice in our circumstances* (This is what we often call open and closed doors.) Reading the circumstances when it comes to life choices requires discernment. How do I know if this is God trying to block me from something outside His perfect plan or the devil trying to keep me from the center of God's will? This is where the other three components of the guidance-processing matrix prove very helpful. If everything else points to God at work except the circumstances, it is much easier to read who is holding the door shut.

Personal illustration: About the time all of this started to make sense, the board of EYL initiated major changes resulting from several years of financial pressure. Very few situations in my leadership journey have been so littered with teachable moments. The bottom line is my circumstances began to validate the decisions I felt needed to be made.

I found myself in the midst of a major personal change-management process. Yet I had beneath me the assurance of God's leading through His Word (I only gave you one of several examples), within me the peace that only God can give, around me the safety of a multitude of counselors, and before me the open doors of God's guiding hand.

WORKING IT OUT

Ideas for Application and Reflection

Think back to the last "life choice" you had to make. Think over the following questions in light of that decision.

1. What guidance-processing format did you use? Did it serve you well?

2. How readily could you explain that process to someone you are mentoring?

3. How confident are the people who follow you as it relates to your ability to hear God's voice? How do you know?

After reflecting on the above consider the following:

1. Do a teaching session in a small group or Sunday school class on guidance processing. Let me know what date you plan to do it so I can pray for you.

2. Share with one of your mentees a principle you have learned from the reflection questions above.

3. Contact someone you respect and ask him or her how they process "life choices."

24 The Focused Life

> **"A weak man with an ax can cut more wood than a strong man with a sledgehammer."**

Merely working harder at what you are currently doing may not provide the payoff you could get by sharpening your tool. If the "tool" in question is your life, the process of being sharpened can be described as living a focused life. A Gallup study documented in the book *Now, Discover Your Strengths* found that "excellent performers were rarely well rounded. On the contrary, they were sharp." A weak man with an ax can cut more wood than a strong man with a sledgehammer.

The technical definition of a focused life is *a life dedicated to exclusively carrying out God's unique purposes by identifying the focal issues, which allow an increasing prioritization of life's activities (around these focal issues) resulting in a satisfying life of being and doing.* (This is a *Leadership Emergence Theory* concept that is developed in Dr. J. Robert Clinton's book *Strategic Concepts that Clarify a Focused Life.*)

Steps Toward a Focused Life

There are four important components of a focused life. (These are my interpretations of Dr. Clinton's concepts—translating "Clintonese" into a language younger leaders can speak and understand.)

- *Dedication*—The first step in moving toward a focused life is being dedicated exclusively to carrying out God's unique purposes. Every leader who has been sharpened into an ax and swung by the hands of God began with a willful choice to dedicate himself or herself totally to God. This commitment is of course renewed many times in the course of life and ministry, but it has to start somewhere. More

> ❝ **You don't need to know anything about giftedness or destiny to climb on the altar and die to selfish ambition.** ❞

than any other issue, young leaders can be encouraged to pursue this kind of total abandonment to God. You don't need to know anything about your giftedness or destiny to climb on the altar and die to selfish ambition, embracing the purposes of God for your life. Are you totally dedicated to carrying out His purposes?

- *Identification*—The second step toward a focused life is identifying the focal issues. Rarely will there be any significant progress toward this goal until the first step has been taken—that of dedicating oneself completely to God's purposes. There are four focal elements in a focused life as follows:

  —*Life Purpose:* Life purpose deals with the missional essence of one's life. It answers the fundamental question "Why am I here?" I believe the highest expression of destiny awareness is a cohesive personal life mission statement.

  —*Effective Methods:* Knowing your mission is not enough. You will need a growing set of effective methods, skills, and spiritual gifts to fulfill the mission God has mapped out for you. And if you are a young leader, you probably have not developed many of these skills and gifts. As ministry leaders move along a continuum of giftedness discovery, they begin to acquire a basic set of effective methods which enable them to carry out their mission (even if the mission is at an entirely implicit or embryonic stage.) These become the "favorite tools" in the ministry leader's toolbox that enable repeated and increased ministry effectiveness.

  —*Major Role:* Eventually ministry leaders sense the need for a major role to serve as the platform upon which their effective methods can be employed to accomplish the life mission they have embraced. This major role usually brings an increasing overlap of passions, giftedness, and responsibilities.

—*Ultimate Contributions:* The lifetime legacy or cumulative fruitfulness of a ministry leader in various streams of service can be described in terms of categories of ultimate contribution to the Kingdom. This is in some sense the ministry expression of "beginning with the end in mind" principle.

The process of identification in living a focused life involves the uncovering of these focal elements. The more focal elements identified, the more focus a leader will achieve.

- *Prioritization*—The third step in living a focused life is intentionally prioritizing the activities of life around the growing understanding of these focal elements. It is one thing to know them; it is another step altogether to act accordingly. Leaders moving toward a focused life are proactive about refining their understanding of life purpose. They intentionally cultivate growth patterns that expand the base of effective methods. They carefully balance the need to submit and serve with the desire to carve out a major role. They poise themselves for the moment of risk and adventure when that major role will need to be embraced. They seek to identify the threads of ultimate contribution and proactively filter major projects based on how they will contribute to the tapestry that will be crafted by their lasting legacy.

- *Satisfaction*—The final step of a focused life is a satisfied life of being and doing. Focus provides a measure of unique ministry fulfillment. This is not to say that leaders who do not experience focus know nothing of ministry fulfillment. But leaders who live a focused life accomplish more of what God intended and in turn experience a deeper level of satisfaction as expressed by Jesus himself who said, "I have brought you glory on the earth by completing the work you gave me to do" (John 17:4).

A focused life cannot be cultivated overnight. While there is no set timetable for obtaining focus, the sharpening process usually unfolds in the following timetable:

Age 30–40

Priority Focus: Identification (Life Purpose refinement, Effective Methods refinement with intimation of Major Role and Ultimate Contributions)

Secondary Focus: Prioritization

Age 40–50

Priority Focus: Identification (Major Role—usually beginning at age 40, Ultimate Contribution awareness)

Secondary Focus: Prioritization

Age 50–60

Priority Focus: Prioritization

Secondary Focus: Identification (Ultimate Contribution refinement)

Age 60+

Priority Focus: Prioritization

Final Comments

The first stage is not a function of skills or training. It is a heart level commitment leaders must make. The prioritization stage is meaningless without an awareness of the four key concepts that flow from the identification stage. Satisfaction will take care of itself. Therefore, the most important way to help leaders move toward a focused life is by addressing the key concepts in stage two—identification.

WORKING IT OUT

Ideas for Application and Reflection

1. Leaders who have dealt with the first step toward a focused life tend to remember a crisis moment when they unconditionally dedicated themselves to God with the intent of carrying out His unique purpose. Do you remember when you first made this kind of commitment? If you have never done so, write a short narrative in a journal format describing this time of dedication and reaffirm it before God.

2. Which of the four focal elements do you most need to identify based on season of life in which you find yourself? How can you work on identifying this focal element?

3. Many young leaders deal with impatience as they discover the principles of a focused life. Share what you are learning with an accountability partner, and ask them to hold you accountable in this area.

4. Pick your favorite historical mentor and evaluate them in terms of focused living. Try to discover where in their life they processed each of the four stages. What can you learn from their journey?

Top Flight Leadership

The Pioneer in Experience-Based Young Leader Development

Top Flight Leadership is committed to developing young leaders through training experiences and resource development. Our vision is to see new generations of leaders all over the world empowered for a lifetime of Kingdom-advancing ministry. We accomplish this through a variety of training opportunities including:

Customized Training Events

Top Flight Leadership will work with you to identify the needs of your young leaders and then provide training customized to help your leadership grow and excel.

Charting the Course

A powerful leadership experience that helps young leaders discover their personal life destiny and develop a life plan.

Road Map

Practical training helping organizational and ministry leaders clarify vision, mission, and core values; build a team; and engage in effective strategic planning.

Focused Living

Focused Living will help young leaders live life with focus as they embrace life planning, growth planning, role planning, and legacy planning.

Epic Revolution

Experience-based leadership training for junior- and senior-high students that helps them increase their influence by building character, overcoming challenges, and developing leadership skills.

EuroTrain

The ultimate experience that takes high school and college-age young leaders on a leadership adventure throughout Europe.

New leadership experiences are always in development.

For more information visit

www.topflight.org

or contact us at
Top Flight Leadership
PO Box 330517 Ft. Worth, TX 76163

817-568-2711
or toll free at 866-9-LEADER (953-2337)

Top Flight Leadership

Focused Living Leadership Experience

Focused Living is a leadership experience designed to help young leaders maximize their Kingdom impact. This experience focuses on four components:

- Life Planning—Discover your life purpose
- Growth Planning—Develop leadership and ministry skills
- Role Planning—Define your ideal role
- Legacy Planning—Determine your lasting legacy

The Focused Living leadership experience is offered in three different formats:

1. One Hour: Focused Living Overview Module

This is a one-hour module that introduces participants to the four components and gives them a basic understanding of how each one helps leaders live a focused life.

2. One Weekend: Focused Living Leadership Experience

The weekend experience takes participants deeper into the four components of focused living. They will deepen their understanding of what it means to live a focused life and how to embrace life planning, growth planning, role planning, and legacy planning in a more intentional manner.

3. One Year: Focused Living Coaching Experience

The Focused Living Coaching Experience includes four Modules spread out over one year and combines integrated resources, personal coaching, group interaction, Life Mapping Retreat, and a Focused Living Follow-up Network that will enable you to:

- Discover your life purpose (Module 1: Life Planning)
- Develop leadership and ministry skills (Module 2: Growth Planning)
- Define your ideal role (Module 3: Role Planning)
- Determine your lasting legacy (Module 4: Legacy Planning)

You will come away from your Focused Living Coaching Experience with a Life Map that includes a working draft of your personal life mission, a growth plan outlining the effective methods you will need to fulfill that purpose, a description of the roles or team context in which you could most efficiently apply these effective methods, and a basic outline of the ultimate contributions you will leave behind as the core of your lasting legacy.

Learn more about Focused Living by visiting
www.topflight.org
or calling Top Flight Leadership at 866-9-LEADER (953-2337)

Top Flight Leadership

Resources

Developing Student Leaders is a complete resource designed to help you build student leaders within your ministry. This resource comes complete with keys to developing student leaders, steps to building a leadership team, insights to the long-term growth of student leaders, practical application worksheets, an appendix full of leadership tools, and four powerful leadership lessons that can be used in training your student leaders. $20 (plus shipping & handling)

Student Leadership 101 is the companion resource to *Developing Student Leaders*. This 64-page booklet contains outlines to each of the four lessons in *Developing Student Leaders* including Foundations of Christian Leadership, Expectations & Responsibilities of Student Leaders, The Seven Greatest Downfalls of Young Leaders, and Understanding Teamwork. Each outline allows students to fill-in-the-blanks as youth leaders teach the material. In addition, outlines are followed by a assessment and action step worksheets and insights from other leaders. $5 (plus shipping & handling)

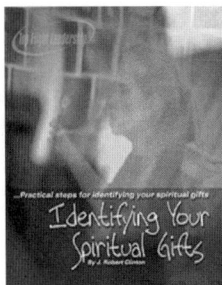

Identifying Your Spiritual Gifts is a young-leader friendly spiritual gifts assessment tool. It includes two audio teachings, notes and outlines, and a 20-copy license of the assessment tool. This practical resource will help young leaders take steps toward the discovery of their spiritual gifts.
$25 (plus shipping & handling)

Order online at
www.topflight.org
or by calling toll-free
866-9-LEADER (953-2337)
Credit Cards Accepted

Top Flight Leadership

eCentre for Young Leader Training

Are you looking for online leadership training that fits your schedule?

Do you need leadership training that personalized?

Are searching for practical training that connects you with other young leaders?

The eCentre is Your Answer!

Through the eCentre you now have online access to a growing reservoir of interactive, experience-based, ministry-focused leadership training that is geared specifically for young leaders. What's different about eCentre learning adventures?

- They're personalized so you can customize the content to suit your goals.
- They're flexible so they fit your priorities and schedule—not ours.
- They're relational so you can connect and interact with other young leaders.
- They're experiential so you can apply them to real life.
- They are affordable, allowing you to grow your leadership without breaking your budget.

To learn more about the eCentre, visit us online at

www.topflight.org

or

www.ecentrelearning.org

Top Flight Leadership

e-zines

LEADERSHIP MINUTE
A Top Flight Leadership publication

Leadership Minute is a free monthly leadership email sent to young leaders around the world. This quick-read leadership publication includes an introduction to a relevant leadership topic, and a brief book review. *Leadership Minute* is published twice per month. You can sign up online at www.topflight.org.

LEADERSHIP INSIGHTS ONLINE
A Top Flight Leadership publication

Leadership Insights is a much more expanded and in-depth leadership email. This resource is published twice per month and includes an in-depth leadership article, practical application tips, a thorough book review that includes a book summary, best price online, quotes, best chapter, and best illustration, and a 10 percent discount on all Top Flight products. By purchasing this book, you will receive a free six-month trial subscription at no cost (a $12 value). To begin receiving your new subscription, follow the instructions on the label inside the back cover of this book.